AF529289

WTO and India

Challenges and Opportunities

WTO and India

Challenges and Opportunities

Ravishankar Kumar Singh
R. Shashi Kumar

ABHIJEET PUBLICATIONS
DELHI 110094

ABHIJEET PUBLICATIONS
2/46 Tukhmeerpur Extension
Delhi 110094
Phones: 011-22960492, 65698474
e-mail: abhijeetpublication@gmail.com
abhijeet_singh1@indiatimes.com

WTO AND INDIA: CHALLENGES AND OPPORTUNITIES

First Published 2008

© Reserved

ISBN 978-81-89886-70-7

[All rights reserved. No part of this publication may be reproduced, copied, stored in a retrieval system, transmitted or used in any form or by any means, whether electronic, mechanical, photocopying, recording or otherwise, without the prior permission from the author or publisher, except for a brief quotations in critical articles or reviews. The onus of establishing authenticity and originality is entirely with the contributors. The publisher and Editors are in no way responsible for the facts and views expressed by the contributors.]

PRINTED IN INDIA

Published bv J.K. Singh for Abhijeet Publications, Delhi 110094, Lasertypeset by Gaurav Graphics, Delhi and Printed at Himanshu Printers, Delhi.

PREFACE

The signing of the GATT accord by 120 countries at Marrakesh on the 15th of April, 1994 is possibly the greatest endeavour towards human accord in the second half of the Twentieth Century just as the founding of the United Nations was the greatest achievement of the first half of this century. Thus, establishment of the World Trade Organisation (WTO) which is the embodiment of the result of Uruguay Round held during a long period of about eight years from 1986 to 1994, is possibly a mighty big event in international economic scenario. This new apex body equipped with the legal authority and provisions for enforcing the commitments, rules and norms came into existence on 1st January, 1995. It professes trade liberalisation through an open, rule-based and non-discriminatory multilateral trading system which provides greater trade flows for ail its participating members thereby ensuring fair distribution of the fruits of global economic development. This young institution having 148 countries as its members at present and governing 95% of the global trade emerged as the third economic pillar of worldwide dimension next to the IMF and the IBRD. This biggest international trading organisation helps in implementing the past negotiations, initiating periodic review of the trade policy and settling the trade disputes among its member countries. Evolution of a free trading environment for the movement of goods and services is its objective based on the assumption that free trade is an optimal modality of global welfare. The underlying principles of the WTO are transparency and provision by member of national treatment and most favoured nation treatment to all the members. It is 'the best basis and perhaps the only basis for establishing and maintaining a bilateral world trade order with a system of international legal constraints trade policies under the MFN Principle' (WTO Report, 1995).

In this book, the scholars present their diverse and deep analytical, sometimes critical, viewpoints on WTO as an organisation presenting challenges and offering development and growth opportunities to India. The effects of WTO on Indian economy, services, agriculture, manufacturing, small scale industries, multinational corporations, exports, foreign direct investment etc. all have been studied by our scholars as well. As there is ongoing tussle between developed and developing countries in WTO, especially led by Commerce Minister Mr. Kamal Nath, this book while covering this issue also makes Indian standpoint very clear.

It is hoped that this book will prove useful to the students and scholars of Indian Economy.

Ravishankar Kumar Singh
R. Shashi Kumar

CONTENTS

1

INTRODUCTION

*R.K. Singh & R. Shashi Kumar**

PART I
WORLD TRADING SYSTEM

1.1 Introduction

Trillions of dollars worth of investments, capital flows, goods and services now make their way around the world economy. With the new opportunities, come new risks and powerful reasons for policy-makers to worry about globalization and its impact. The new global economy is the product of three changes: internationalization, liberalization, and a technological revolution. Internationalization has been occurring over a long period of time as states forge more links with one another as well as more international institutions to pursue mutual goals. Liberalization has accelerated since the 1980s with governments the world over adopting policies which integrate their economies more closely into the world economy. For some countries this is more of a genuine `choice' than for others who have liberalized under intense pressure from bilateral donors, and international institutions such as the WTO, the IMF and the World Bank. A revolution in technology and communications has fuelled change, making it easier for market actors, companies, nongovernmental organizations and the like—not to mention criminal gangs—to operate

* Reader in Economics, Department of Economics, Bangalore University, Bangalore—560 056, Karnataka State, India.

transnationally. The product is a world economy in which policy-makers and their constituencies are less sure of what can be managed in the world economy and how.

1.2 WTO and World Trade

Ever since it's founding in January 1995, the World Trade Organization has been the focus of global protest. While its defenders claim that it is intended to spread the world's wealth through lower tariffs, its detractors insist it is a tool of the United States and other wealthy nations, serving to widen the gap between the world's rich and poor.

The World Trade Organization came into being in 1995. One of the youngest of the international organizations, the WTO is the successor to the General Agreement on Tariffs and Trade (GATT) established in the wake of the Second World War. So while the WTO is still young, the multilateral trading system that was originally set up under GATT is well over 50 years old. The past 50 years have seen an exceptional growth in world trade. Merchandise exports grew on average by 6 percent annually. Total trade in 1997 was 14-times the level of 1950. GATT and the WTO have helped to create a strong and prosperous trading system contributing to unprecedented growth. The system was developed through a series of trade negotiations, or rounds, held under GATT. The first rounds dealt mainly with tariff reductions but later negotiations included other areas such as anti-dumping and non-tariff measures. The last round–the 1986-94 Uruguay Round–led to the WTO's creation. The negotiations did not end there. Some continued after the end of the Uruguay Round. In February 1997 agreement was reached on telecommunications services, with 69 governments agreeing to wide-ranging liberalization measures that went beyond those agreed in the Uruguay Round. In the same year 40 governments successfully concluded negotiations for tariff-free trade in information technology products, and 70 members concluded a financial services deal covering more than 95 per cent of trade in banking, insurance, securities and financial information.

In 2000, new talks started on agriculture and services.

These have now been incorporated into a broader work programme, the Doha Development Agenda (DDA), launched at the fourth WTO Ministerial Conference in Doha, Qatar, in November 2001. The agenda adds negotiations and other work on non-agricultural tariffs, trade and environment, WTO rules such as anti-dumping and subsidies, investment, competition policy, trade facilitation, transparency in government procurement, intellectual property, and a range of issues raised by developing countries as difficulties they face in implementing the present WTO agreements.

1.3 Background to WTO Negotiations

In the period immediately following World War II, three organizations were set up to monitor international trade and payments. Since these organizations or building blocks emerged as a result of a UN-sponsored conference held in 1944 in a place known as Bretton Woods, the system that emerged was known as the Bretton Woods system. The first two organizations were the International Monetary Fund (IMF) and the International Bank for Reconstruction and Development (IBRD), popularly known as the World Bank. The third organization that was supposed to be set was something known as the International Trade Organization (ITO). ITO was never actually set up. Instead, one had something known as the General Agreement on Tariffs and Trade (GATT). Unlike ITO, had it actually been set up, GATT was only a legal agreement. It was not a proper organization.

GATT's mandate was to liberalize world trade. Barriers to world trade can be of two types - tariffs and non-tariff barriers (NTBs). Tariffs work through prices, that is, they jack up the cost of imports through customs duties. NTBs are not price-based. Examples are import licensing or quotas. They also restrict imports, but not through increasing prices of such imports. As is understandable, unlike tariffs, NTBs are difficult to monitor, police, or even quantify. GATT seeks to address its mandate through a series of negotiations known as multilateral trade negotiations (MTNs). Every once in a while, GATT members come together and decide that a mutually acceptable liberalization package will be implemented. These negotiations are also known as MTN rounds. So far, eight such MTN rounds have taken place—Geneva (1947), Annecy (1949), Torquay (1951), Geneva (1956), Geneva (1960-61, also known as the Dillon Round), Geneva (1964-67, also known as the Kennedy Round), Geneva (1973-79, also known as the Tokyo Round) and Geneva (1984-96, also known as the Uruguay Round).

At the first round in Geneva in 1947, 23 countries participated and these were founder-members of GATT, India being a founder-member. At the Uruguay Round, the number of participating countries was 123, although the number of WTO (World Trade Organization) members has now gone up to 148. More than 92 per cent of world trade now takes place among WTO members. Several countries (such as former socialist countries) are waiting to become members of WTO and the waiting list has more than thirty aspirants. Once these entries take place, perhaps around 98 percent of world trade will take place among WTO members.

When GATT was supposed to liberalize world trade, it was supposed to eliminate both tariffs and NTBs. In fact, GATT has been quite successful in reducing tariffs all around the globe. But because NTBs are much more difficult to pin down, GATT's success in eliminating NTBs has been much more limited. However, once tariffs began to come down, the focus shifted to eliminating NTBs. The Kennedy Round is roughly when this focus shifted and the Tokyo Round had several agreements on NTBs. Perhaps one should also mention that GATT was ostensibly supposed to look at external sector policies. But as international trade and business became much more complicated, it became difficult to differentiate external sector policies from domestic economic policies.[1]

There were three new areas that were discussed for the first time in the course of the Uruguay Round-trade-related investment measures (TRIMs), trade-related intellectual property rights (TRIPs) and services.[2]

1.3.1 *Major Uruguay Round agreements*

The following are the major Uruguay Round Agreements:

- Agreement on Agriculture

- Agreement on Sanitary and Phytosanitary Measures (SPS)
- Agreement on Textiles and Clothing
- Agreement on Technical Barriers to Trade (TBT)
- Agreement on Trade Related Investment Measures (TRIMs)
- Agreement on Article VI of GATT (Anti-Dumping)
- Understanding on the Balance of Payments
- Understanding on the Rules and Procedures Governing the Settlement of Disputes (DSU)
- Agreement on Subsidies and Countervailing Measures
- Agreement on Trade Related Aspects of Intellectual Property Rights (TRIPs)
- General Agreement on Trade in Services (GATS)

1.3.2 The Doha Development Agenda (DDA) and Subsequcnt Ministerials

The Uruguay Round (1986-94) negotiations led to the inclusion of services and TRIPs in multilateral trade negotiations and also incorporated liberalization of agriculture and textiles and garments within goods agreements. And from 1st January 1995, the historical General Agreement on Tariffs and Trade (GATT), which was really a General Agreement on Goods (GATG), was subsumed under the WTO (World Trade Organization). Other than GATG, WTO administers the General Agreement on Trade in Services (GATS) and the TRIPs agreement, the latter through a TRIPs Council. The agreement setting up the WTO requires a Ministerial Conference to be held once every two years.

The first Ministerial Conference was held in Singapore in 1996, which is how the Singapore issues of trade facilitation, transparency in government procurement, competition policy and investment obtain their name. The second Ministerial Conference was held in Geneva in 1998. The third Ministerial Conference in Seattle in 1999 was extremely controversial, because it was expected to announce the launch of a new round of WTO negotiations, known at that time as the

Millennium Round. The agenda of the Millennium Round became controversial, with developing countries focusing on market access liberalization and developed countries focusing on newer areas like the Singapore issues. The Seattle Conference failed to launch a new round. And it was left to the fourth Ministerial Conference in Doha in 2001 to launch the DDA (Doha Development Agenda).

1.4 Developing Countries and International

1.4.1 Development and Trade

Over three quarters of WTO members are developing or least developed countries. All WTO agreements contain special provision for them, including longer time periods to implement agreements and commitments, measures to increase their trading opportunities, provisions requiring all WTO members to safeguard their trade interests, and support to help them build the infrastructure for WTO work, handle disputes, and implement technical standards.

The 2001 Ministerial Conference in Doha set out tasks, including negotiations, for a wide range of issues concerning developing countries. Some people call the new negotiations the Doha Development Round. Before that, in 1997, a high-level meeting on trade initiatives and technical assistance for least-developed countries resulted in an "integrated framework" involving six intergovernmental agencies, to help least-developed countries increase their ability to trade, and some additional preferential market access agreements. A WTO committee on trade and development, assisted by a subcommittee on least-developed countries, looks at developing countries' special needs. Its responsibility includes implementation of the agreements, technical cooperation, and the increased participation of developing countries in the global trading system.

1.4.2 Technical Assistance and Training

The WTO organizes around 100 technical cooperation missions to developing countries annually. It holds on average three trade policy courses each year in Geneva for government officials. Regional seminars are held regularly in all regions of the world with a special emphasis on African countries. Training courses are also organized in Geneva for officials from countries in transition from central planning to market economies. The WTO set up reference centers in over 100 trade ministries and regional organizations in capitals of developing and least-developed countries, providing computers and internet access to enable ministry officials to keep abreast of events in the WTO in Geneva through online access to the WTO's immense database of official documents and other material.

1.5 The Review of Literature

Trade liberalisation embraces all the elements in the opening of markets and can have one or several of these ingredients. There may be a reduction in tariffs and non-tariff barriers, a relaxation of investment and capital flows between countries and an enhanced transparency of trade policies and trade facilitation measures. Trade liberalisation in a broad sense argues for measures that facilitate an increase in trade and does not necessarily imply free movement of factors of production such as labour and capital.

The pro-liberalisation lobby has two strong proponents (Bhagwati, 2004; Wolf, 2004; Bhagwati and Kreuger, 1974) who strongly argue that globalization and outward-oriented policies contribute to sustained economic growth. Panagariya (2004) has found that the growth miracle countries that grew at a rate of 3 per cent per capita or more on a sustained basis between 1961 and 1999 almost always experienced a rapid growth in trade. Moreover, there are few examples of highly-protected countries that managed to grow rapidly on a sustained basis without lowering their level of protection. Countries that have failed to grow had a dismal trade performance. Some serious advocates of free trade argue that openness is by itself sufficient for growth. They are aware that macroeconomic stability, the enforcement of contracts and policy credibility are necessary to register significantly higher economic growth.

Among the free trade sceptics, Rodriguez and Rodrik (1999) provide a critique of the link between growth and openness. Cross-country regression studies provide weak evidence on the relationship between openness and growth. The South Centre of the United Nations raises severe doubts about the benefits of liberalisation and globalisation and remains critical of the World Bank studies, which according to the Centre are based on a misinterpretation of the facts. Liberalisation and globalisation have progressed at a slower pace in developing countries as compared with advanced countries.

Wacziarg and Welch (2003) have constructed a panel data set on income growth and liberalisation, which allowed them to identify both within country and between country variations. They find that, on average, a country grows at a set 1.5 per cent per annum higher rate in the liberalized phase than in the protected phase, controlling for country and year effects on the panel data. While assessing the impact of openness on growth, real exchange rate policy is very important. If the real exchange rate is left overvalued when countries liberalize, it maintains the discrimination against traded goods. This would obviously reduce the impact of openness on growth. Stiglitz (2002) raises issues about the speed of liberalisation. His argument rests on two main considerations, namely, that trade liberalisation must be gradual and developed countries need to do their part by removing trade barriers on products of interest to developing countries, especially agriculture, where domestic and export subsidies further harm the interests of developing countries.

Winters (2004) concludes that openness to trade boosts economic growth rates in developing countries but not for ever. He claims that when a country opens up by reducing tariffs and removing other barriers, economic growth increases for a period while incomes climb to their new higher level but then settle back to the underlying rate. Open economies seem to have less corruption and lower inflation, and these factors, along with opportunities to sell goods abroad, help growth by stimulating investment. Since openness promotes investment, it is clearly the engine of economic growth. Trade liberalisation and sound finances obviously go together. Dollar and Kraay (2004) have examined the impact of openness which they called "globalisation" and examined its impact on economic growth, poverty and inequality in a large number of developing countries.

1.6 Plan of the Study

As far as trade liberalization is concerned under the WTO, the purpose of this paper is to show the fallacies and contradictions surrounding the concepts and practices of universal trade liberalization and protection. The main fallacies are related to: *(i)* the philosophy behind universal and across-the-board trade liberalization; *(ii)* contradictions in the design and implementation of agreed rules during the various rounds of trade negotiations under GATT and in the positions of some groups in their implementation; *(iii)* the theory of protection of infant industry; *(iv)* and, in particular, perceptions about the interests of developed countries in universal and across-the-board trade liberalization. In this background, the paper is divided into three parts. The first part provides introduction to the world trading system. The second part summarizes the recent events since the conclusion of the Uruguay Round Agreement (URA). Part three will present some conclusions outlining policy implications and present some recommendations.

It should be emphasized from the outset that, as will be explained later in this paper, free trade under the WTO should be the ultimate aim of every nation once all economies have reached similar level of development. Hence, the content of this study should not be interpreted as expressing views against that "ultimate" aim.

PART II
THE WORLD TRADE SCENARIO

Stronger industrial activity was mirrored in world trade. Merchandise trade growth grew 11 per cent during the first eight months of 2006, up from 6 per cent the year before. Most of the acceleration occurred in China, Japan, and the United States and was concentrated in the first quarter. Weaker U.S. consumption and investment demand, and growing domestic demand in the developing world combined with the lagged effects of past depreciations to boost U.S. export volumes by an annualized rate of 13 per cent in the first half of 2006, compared with 7 per cent in the last half of 2005. Measured on the same basis and over the same period, exports in Japan and China increased by 10 and 30 per cent, respectively. Trade flows weakened in the second quarter but show signs of picking up once again in the third quarter.

2.1 Trade and Developed Countries

Trade among developed countries is explained by increasing return to scale and/or product differentials. In theory, a distinction is made between two types of scale economies: those internal to the firm and those external it.[3] Nevertheless, the literature is not always clear with respect to the interrelation between increasing return and international trade, as the concept of increasing return is a complex one. Scale economies can be static or dynamic, they can be internal or external to an operational unit, and could be at various levels. They can be product-specific, plant-specific, firm-specific or industry-specific. One could think of scale economies at the level of the manufacturing sector as a whole. One may also distinguish national economies from international ones at the level of industry. The sources of scale economies are also diverse; they may be not only at the production level, but also in marketing and distribution, management and control and R&D.

The emergence and development of mega firms has an important economic reason with its significant implications for the international trade of developing countries. The rationale for mergers is basically more important. Moreover, the importance of brand names, and marketing and advertisement in the cost structure has increased. All these activities, particularly R&D, involve significant economies of scale internal economies of scale at the firm level. More recently, the production process in both industrial and services sector is becoming more and more knowledge-based.

Over the medium term, growth in merchandise trade volumes is projected to ease to about 9 per cent, in line with slower global GDP growth. The recent relative strength of U.S. export volumes is projected to persist (figure 1). Those volumes are projected to raise by more than 9 percent in 2007 and 2008 as the cumulative effect of past and expected future depreciations increase the international competitiveness of U.S. products. For developing countries, weaker U.S. import demand should be partially compensated by stronger demand from Europe, but, overall, developing country export growth is projected to slow from an estimated 12.2 per cent in 2006 to 10 percent in 2008, even as countries continue to increase their market share.

Figure 1. Rotation in Global Trade, Merchandise Trade Volumes

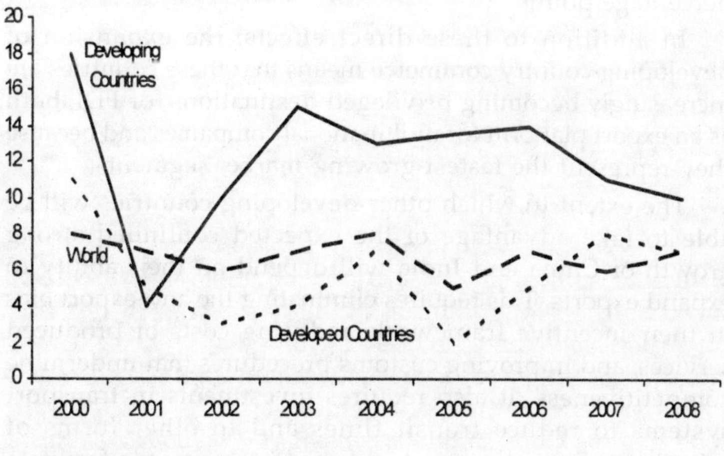

Source: World Bank.

2.2 Trade Outlook—Continued Expansion

Developing-country trade reached a landmark in 2006. Following 25 years of solid growth, the value of China's exports overtook those of the United States, making China the world's second-largest exporter. Increasing exports in other developing countries, notably Brazil and India, have further increased the weight of developing countries in world trade. Over the long term, as these trends continue, the share of developing countries in world trade is projected to reach some 45 per cent by 2030.

While the phenomenal success that China has enjoyed in expanding its world market share since the introduction of market reforms has increased competitive pressure on both developing and developed countries, Chinese imports also have grown very rapidly (up 477 per cent in value terms over the past decade), and China is a growing destination for the exports of other developing countries. Sixty-three percent of China's imports are intermediate goods, 31 percent in the form of parts and components. Overall, 79 percent of China's imports are sourced from developing countries. Partly as a result of China's rapid increase in imports, the value of other developing countries' non-oil exports has risen by 153 per cent, and their global market share has increased by 2.3 percentage points.

In addition to these direct effects, the expansion of developing-country commerce means that these countries are increasingly becoming privileged destinations for FDI, both as an export platform for multinational companies and because they represent the fastest-growing market segment.

The extent to which other developing countries will be able to take advantage of the expected continued strong growth of China and India will depend on their ability to expand exports. This requires eliminating the anti-export bias in their incentive framework, reducing costs of produced services, and improving customs procedures that undermine competitiveness. It also requires investments in transport systems to reduce transit times and in other forms of infrastructure, such as electrical generators so as to facilitate the expansion of capacity. In addition, countries need to reduce rigidities in product, labor, and financial markets so that firms can react with agility to new opportunities to expand the range of products they produce and sell.

On the multilateral front, the suspension of talks on the Doha Round in July 2006 poses significant challenges. Weakened confidence in the multilateral system could lead to trade disputes, rising protectionist sentiment, and trade diversion arising from proliferating bilateral and regional trade agreements. To capitalize on progress already made in the Doha Round, such as the offer to end agricultural export subsidies by 2013, it is important that parties return to the negotiating table with the necessary flexibility to conclude an ambitious deal.

Since the mid-1990s exports from low income countries and the LDCs have grown faster than the average for the world and for developing countries (see table 1). This largely reflects an increase in commodity prices and more recently the decline in the U.S. dollar, as well as an increase in exports of manufactures (textiles). These developments contributed to a minor recovery in these countries' world market shares, though these remain below those of the 1970s. Global export shares for low-income African countries and for the LDCs as a group exceed their shares in world GDP. Average import growth rates have also picked up recently for low-income countries and the LDCs, outpacing growth in imports for the world and for developing countries during 2001–07.

Table 1: Applied Most Favoured Nation Tariffs are Highest in South Asia and Sub-Saharan Africa (Simple Average, Percent)

Region/Income Group	*Late 1980s*	*2007 (Preliminary)*
East Asia	18.8	9.6
Europe and Central Asia	10.2	7.3
Latin America and the Caribbean	22.4	10.4
Middle East and North Africa	17.3	12.4
South Asia	68.9	17.7
Sub-Saharan Africa	25.1	15.3
High-income OECD	7.0	4.1
High-income non-OECD	9.0	6.6

Developing Countries	25.4	11.7
Least developed countries	28.4	15.1
Low-income countries	31.7	12.9
Middle-income countries	21.8	10.5

Sources: UNCTAD TRAINS database; World Bank, World Development Indicators; IMF Trade Policy Information Database; WTO Trade Policy Reviews.

Note: Classification of regions and income groups based on World Bank 2006b.

2.2.1 Tariffs, Nontariff Measures, and Contingent Protection

In recent years there has been a decline in tariff barriers worldwide, reflecting autonomous reform, regional agreements, and WTO accession (including by Cambodia, China, Egypt, India, Iran, Pakistan, Tunisia, and Zimbabwe). Globally, average tariffs fell by 2 percentage points between 1997 and 2000 and by 1 point between 2000 and 2007. As measured by MFN requirements that apply in principle to both imports and domestic products; see below.) Nontariff measures apply to a large share of trade, with the highest ratios in developing countries (table 2).

Table 2 Non-tariff Measures Remain High in Several Regions, 2006 (Per cent)

Region/Income Group	*Frequency Ratio (share of tariff lines)*	*Coverage Ratio (share of imports)*
East Asia	44.0	32.8
Europe and Central Asia	14.6	23.9
Latin America and the Caribbean	26.9	44.4
Middle East and North Africa	49.5	51.6
South Asia	12.1	28.6
Sub-Saharan Africa	24.4	28.8
High-income OECD	22.0	24.1
High-income non-OECD	45.1	46.9
Developing Countries	27.2	34.3
Least developed countries	20.0	36.7
Low-income countries	25.5	36.4
Middle-income countries	28.3	34.0

Sources: UNCTAD TRAINS database; WTO Trade Policy Reviews; EU Product Standards Database; Group d'Economie Mondiale, Institut d'Etudes Politiques.

Note: Classification of regions and income groups based on World Bank 2006b. Nontariff measure price controls, quantify restrictions, state trading monopolies, and technical product regulations as classified in the UNCTAD TRAINS database.

But as discussed below, when converted to advalorem equivalents, nontariff measures are more important in rich countries. The use of instruments of contingent protection—antidumping and safeguard actions—against imports by WTO members has grown steadily, with more than 2,400 antidumping investigations launched since1995 (table 3).

Table 3: Developing Countries Initiate More Antidumping Investigations, 1995-2007

Initiating region	*Target Region*			
	Developed Countries	*Developing Countries*	*Transitional Economies*	*Total*
Developed Countries	226	574 (129)	132	932
Developing Countries	453	827 (225)	173	1,453
Transition Economies	4	7 (2)	20	31
Total	683	1,408 (356)	325	2,416
		Share of total (percent)		
Developed Countries	24.2	61.6 (18.3)	14.2	100.0
Developing Countries	31.2	56.9 (15.5)	11.9	100.0
Transition Economies	12.9	22.6 (6.5)	64.5	100.0
Total (average)	28.3	58.3 (14.7)	13.5	100.0

Source: WTO Antidumping committee data.

Note: Numbers in parentheses are actions against China. Developed counters are Australia, Canada, EU 15, Iceland, Japan, New Zealand, Norway, Switzerland, and United States. Transition economies are Albania, Armenia, Azerbaijan, Belarus, Bosnia and Herzegovina, Bulgaria, Croatia, Czech Republic, Estonia, FYR Maçedonia, Georgia, Hungary, Kazakhstan, Kyrgyz Republic, Latvia, Lithuania, Moldova, Poland, Romania, Russian Federation, Slovak Republic, Slovenia, Tajikistan, Turkmenistan, Ukraine, Uzbekistan, and Yugoslavia.

This instrument is increasingly being used by developing countries against other developing countries. Indeed, developing countries have overtaken developed countries in the number of cases launched: between 2002 and June 2007 developed countries initiated 190 cases, compared with 441 by developing countries. India has passed the United States as the top initiator, and Argentina and South Africa have an even higher incidence of antidumping use relative to the value of their imports (table 4).

Table 4

A Few Large Developing countries have launched the most Antidumping Investigations, 1995-2007

Initiating country/region	*Number of Cases*	*Share of total (percent)*	*Index of initiations per US$ of imports (US=100)*
India	379	15.7	2,416
United State	329	13.6	100
European Union (15)	274	11.3	101
Argentina	180	7.5	2,577
South Africa	166	6.9	2,634
Australia	163	6.7	719
Canada	122	5.0	170
Brazil	109	4.5	590
Mexico	73	3.0	155
China	72	3.0	109

Sources: WTO Antidumping Committee data; IMF, Direction of Trade Statistics.

Another important nontariff measure affecting exports and imports are health and safety related product standards. In contrast to antidumping efforts, which by definition are intended to protect domestic import competing industries, health and safety regulations (mandatory product standards) are often applied equally to domestic and foreign (imported) products—so in principle they are not (or should not be) intended to protect domestic industries. Indeed, WTO rules prohibit the protectionist use of technical product regulations. As discussed below, such norms affect trade by increasing the costs of entering a market, with the incidence of the associated costs differing across countries depending on the composition of their exports and the ease of satisfying (documenting compliance with) a specific norm.

Notwithstanding the rapid rise in commodity prices over the past several years, manufacturing remains the main source of export revenue for developing countries, even when China is excluded from the data (figure 2). If oil exporters are excluded, the result is even stronger, with the overall weight of nonoil commodities falling from 24 per cent to 12 per cent of developing-country (excluding China) exports between 1990 and 2005.

Figure 2
Sources of Export Revenues for Developing Countries

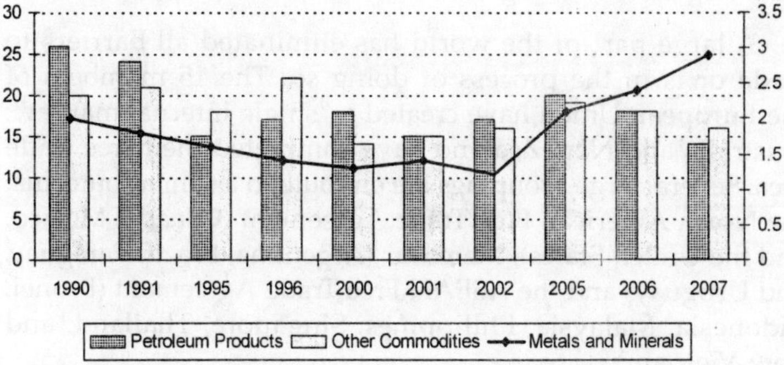

Sources: World Bank; Comtrade.

Note: Figure shows share of commodities in total merchandise export values of developing countries (excluding China).

On the trade policy front, the Doha Round negotiations resumed at the beginning of 2007, following a six-month suspension, partly because of concerns that the United States' fast-track authority would expire and not be renewed. Progress toward sketching an outline of an accord remains limited, however, and a serious risk exists that negotiations will last several years, undermining confidence in the multilateral system. The proliferation of bilateral and regional trade agreements of the kind currently being signed is not a substitute for a multilateral accord, especially because many of the smaller and poorer developing countries are among the least likely to take effective part in them.

For developing countries with a strong specialization in the textiles and clothing sector, the removal of partial restrictions on Chinese exports of these goods to the European Union and the United States in 2008 is expected to dampen export volumes and prices in 2008 and 2009. However, many of these countries have succeeded surprisingly well in the face of the earlier liberalization of the sector in 2006. To the extent that they continue to achieve the kind of efficiency improvement that has underpinned this strong performance, they can be expected to survive this additional pressure relatively well—and indeed, may be well placed to exploit further scale efficiencies.

2.2.2 *Regional Trading Blocs and Trade Improvement*

A large part of the world has eliminated all barriers to trade or is in the process of doing so. The 15 members of the European Union have created a "single internal market". Australia and New Zealand have completed their free trade area. Several large groupings are en route to a similar outcome: the North American Free Trade Agreement (Canada, Mexico, and the United States), Mercosur (Argentina, Brazil, Paraguay, and Uruguay) and the ASEAN Free Trade Agreement (Brunei, Indonesia, Malaysia, Philippines, Singapore, Thailand, and now Vietnam).

In addition, a series of newer groupings have pledged to abolish all impediments to their international trade in the coming years. The European Union and the Mediterranean countries (EUROMED) have committed themselves to free trade by 2010. The 34 democracies of the Western Hemisphere agreed at their Miami summit in December 1994 to work out a Free Trade Area of the Americas (FTAA) by 2005, and negotiations to that end began last spring. The 21 members of the Asia Pacific Economic Cooperation (APEC) forum—which account for half of world output and include the three largest national economies (United States, Japan, and China)—decided via their Bogor Declaration of November 1994 to establish free trade and investment in the region by 2010 for their higher income members, which make up 85 percent of their commerce, and by 2020 for the rest. Over 60 per cent of international commerce now takes place within these existing or planned free trade regimes. This share is rising rapidly, both because of the creation of new arrangements and because trade expands more quickly under such conditions.

Figure 3: Regional Free Trade Arrangements Share of World Trade, 1994

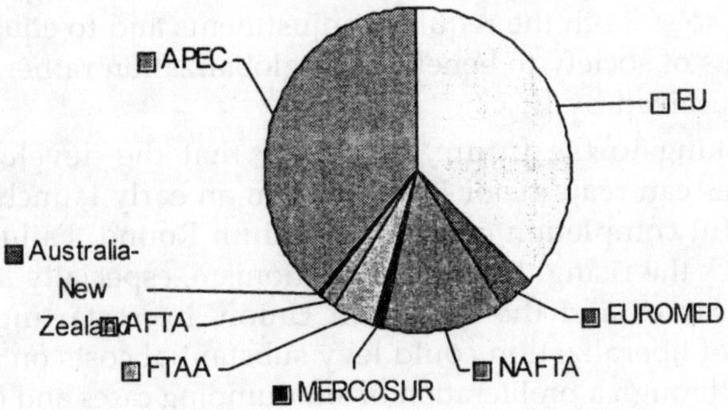

Source: World Bank, 2007.

PART III
IMPLICATIONS OF WTO ON WORLD TRADE

Developing countries clearly reaped important gains from the Uruguay Round of multilateral trade negotiations. World Bank studies, for example, conclude that developing country income levels will rise by 1-2 per cent as a result of the Round and that, as a group, they obtained about one half of its total benefits. The phase-out of the Multifiber Arrangement will provide a substantial boost to their exports. They gain from the total ban on voluntary export restraint agreements (VERs) that was concluded in the Round. The creation of the World Trade Organization (to replace the GATT), and especially its Dispute Settlement Mechanism (DSM), provides substantial protection for countries with smaller levels of trade.

As in any reciprocal negotiation, developing countries of course made several "concessions" in the Uruguay Round. Most of those "concessions," such as reduction in tariffs, in fact benefit their own economies on balance by reducing costs to consumers and to industrial users. Nevertheless, like the United States and all other countries, developing countries experience some costs from trade liberalization and some elements of society may on balance lose from the phenomenon. Hence domestic policy must provide for these contingencies, helping to smooth the required adjustments and to equip all segments of society to benefit from globalization rather than feel victimized by it.

Looking to the future, it is clear that the developing countries can reap major benefits from an early launch and successful completion of the Millennium Round. Failure to turn back the rising threat of protectionism, especially in the United States and the European Union, by restarting the bicycle of liberalization could levy substantial costs on their exports through a proliferation of antidumping cases and other new barriers. It could even jeopardize implementation of the complete phase-out of textile/apparel quotas agreed to in the Uruguay Round. Moreover, a failure to pursue new multilateral liberalization could lead to renewed emphasis by the largest industrial countries, the United States and the European Union, on their regional arrangements. Many developing countries could thus suffer the double loss of renewed barriers and renewed discrimination.

Needless to say, developing countries should vigorously press their own priority interests in pursuing the new Millennium Round. The possibilities include:

- Elimination of the high tariffs that will remain, especially in the United States, on many apparel and textile exports after the phase-out of quotas under the MFA;
- Elimination of the very high tariffs on agricultural imports in many industrialized countries and future reductions in agricultural subsidies;
- Elimination of both tariff escalation and preferential tariffs in regional arrangements, including the EU and NAFTA, that discriminate against exports of many developing countries, by eliminating all tariffs;
- New agreements on foreign direct investment that would both expand its levels and help developing countries achieve a fair share of its benefits, as described above;

- Tougher disciplines on the use of antidumping duties and other safeguard measures, especially by the United States and the European Union;
- Liberalization of movement of natural persons, where many developing countries have a strong competitive advantage, under the General Agreement on Trade in Services; and
- Further strengthening of the DSM to help protect the rights of countries with smaller trade levels.

In short, developing countries have a great deal to gain from a new multilateral round. Pursuing these goals actively would seem to be far preferable to seeking re-negotiation of the Uruguay Round, as some developing countries are considering, which would clearly jeopardize phase-out of the MFA as well as the other gains cited above. Developed countries have an important role to play in providing the resources for the investment needed. This includes direct assistance to facilitate adjustment in those countries badly affected by the loss of preferential margins; and substantial additional resources to allow countries to build a pro-trade infrastructure, and boost their social spending in education and health.

3.1 Myth and Ceremony Trading Practices

Trade policy is at a crossroads. So is trade diplomacy. The failure of the "traditional import substitution" policies of the 1950s-1970s has been followed by the failure of trade liberalization in the 1980s and 1990s by developing countries. In particular, the deadlock in the negotiations during the recent meetings of WTO has demonstrated the severe differences among various groups of member countries. Focusing on frictions between developing countries and industrial economies in the particular area of trade in manufactured goods, the purpose of this paper is to argue that the failure of the negotiations is related to a number of fallacies and contradictions surrounding the concepts and practices of universal trade liberalization and infant industry protection. These main fallacies include: the philosophy behind universal and across-the-board trade liberalization; the contradictions in the design and implementation of GATT/WTO rules to the detrimental interest of developing countries; the theory and practice of infant industry protection; and, in particular, perceptions about the interests of developed countries in universal and across-the-board trade liberalization by developing countries.

Emphasizing that free trade should be the ultimate aim of every nation once all economies have reached similar level of development; it is argued that there is a need for revision of international trade rules. In the design of the new rules more attention should be paid to the level of development and industrial capacity of developing countries. Developing countries should have a clear trade and industrial policy as well as negotiating strategy before entering the negotiation. To play such a proactive role, along the lines suggested in the UNCTAD "Positive Agenda", developing countries should: link their trade policy to their development objective; and follow a dynamic trade policy geared to their level of development, industrial capacity, structural characteristics and changes in the world economy. Moreover, in their common negotiation strategy, instead of agreeing on a "least common denominator", they should attempt to cooperate in elaborating a strategy aiming at the trading rules that differentiate countries, in accordance with some agreed criteria. Such criteria may include a number of indicators, such as per capita income, the degree of dependence on primary commodities, the share of manufacturing in GDP, etc.

Finally, it is a myth to believe that concessions will always be made to developing countries on "moral grounds". Bargaining is the name of the game. Developing countries should mobilize and make the best use of whatever bargaining chips they possess, however small they may be; and developing countries can have some leverage in trade negotiations if they mobilize. Bargaining requires not only bargaining assets, but also knowledge, information about the issues concerned, and training for undertaking trade negotiations. In such a context, at the country level there is a need not only for policy formulation and for strengthening the capacity of commercial diplomacy to enhance bargaining skills, but also for strengthening the capacity for trade and industrial policy formulation and implementation.

3.2 Conclusion

An attempt has been made in this study to discuss some causes of difficulties facing the new round of trade negotiations under the auspices of WTO. The study has focused on frictions between developing and industrialized countries in the particular area of trade in manufactured goods, which is the main concern of developing countries. It was argued that as regards the interests of developing countries, two prime factors have contributed to the failure: fallacies surrounding both the theory of universal and across-the-board trade liberalization, and the theory and practice of infant industry protection- and a contradiction in the design and implementation of GATT and WTO rules to the detriment of the interests of developing countries. It was also shown that rapid and across-the-board liberalization is not in the interest of developed countries- let alone that of developing ones.

Taking into account the prevailing fallacies and contradictions in trade policy theory and practice and bearing in mind the experience of trade policy and diplomacy in recent decades, one is led to conclude that there is a need to design a new trade policy for developing countries as well as to revise international trade rules. In this respect, in preparing themselves for trade negotiations, developing countries need to draw up a clear strategy; the elements of such a strategy could entail the following. First, developing economies need to be clear as to whether they prefer to play a "passive", a "defensive" or a "proactive" role in the negotiations. In the past, they have been passive on some issues and defensive on others. By the latter stance, they opposed what was put on the table by developed countries, as they were either sceptical of the goodwill of the industrialized countries or unsure whether the proposed issue was in their interest. It should be emphasized, however, that negotiation involves a process of give-and-take, which in turn entails bargaining. In bargaining, one needs to play a proactive role.

Secondly, in a proactive role, developing countries both as a group and individually need to adopt a clear position about the type of trade policy they wish to follow—as was stressed by the Secretary-General of UNCTAD in the Positive Agenda for Development. The philosophy behind the "positive agenda" is that instead of opposing whatever is proposed by developed countries in the WTO round of trade negotiations, developing countries should come up with their own trade negotiation agenda. It is maintained that such an agenda should be designed from a development perspective, and that developing countries should make the necessary preparations for the negotiations.

Thirdly, unless they accept being locked in the production and exports of primary commodities, simple processing and "traditional light manufacturing goods" or rather "manufacturing commodities", developing countries need in the long run to have a dynamic trade policy geared to their level of development, industrial capacity and structural characteristics, as well as to changes in world economic conditions and competitive situation.

Fourthly, as each country or group of countries tries to look after its own interests in the process of negotiations, it is a myth to believe that concessions will always be made to developing countries on "moral grounds". "Bargaining" is the name of the game. Bargaining requires bargaining chips, information about the issues under negotiation and bargaining skills. Bargaining chips are the net sum of bargaining assets and liabilities. One should bear in mind that the bargaining chips of developing countries are smaller than those of developed ones. As Dymond and Hart have put it: "The challenge is to look at Seattle as a wake-up call about the object and purpose of post-modern trade policy".[4] Unfortunately, so far this call has not been heard sufficiently by either developing or developed countries although for different reasons.

NOTES

1. Consequently, GATT increasingly began to discuss domestic economic policies and this trend was also clearly visible in the course of the Uruguay Round. This also made negotiations much more complicated and this was one reason why the Uruguay Round negotiations took eight years to be completed.
2. Strictly speaking, there are of course five new areas, since agriculture and textiles and garments were also exempted from GATT disciplines before the Uruguay Round.
3. ETHIER, W.J. (1982). National and International Return to Scale in the Modern Theory of International Trade. *American Economic Review,* June: 388B405.
4. DYMOND, W.A. & HART, M.M. (2000). Post-Modern Trade Policy: Reflections on the Challenges to Multilateral Trade Negotiations after Seattle. *Journal of World Trade Law,* 34 (3) 21-38.

REFERENCES AND FURTHER READINGS

Bhagwati, J. and A. Kreuger (eds.) (1974). *Foreign Trade Regimes and Economic Development: A Special Conference Series on Foreign Trade Regimes and Economic Development,* New York: Cambridge University Press.

Bhagwati, J. (2004). *In Defence of Globalisation,* Oxford: Oxford University Press.

Brahmbhatt, M. and U. Dadush (1996). Disparities in global integration. *Finance and Development,* 33(3), 1–4.

Dollar, D. and A. Kraay (2004). Trade, growth and poverty. *Economic Journal,* 114(493), F22–F49.

Dutta, M. (2006). *China's Industrial Revolution and Economic Presence,* Singapore: World Scientific Publishers.

Feder, G. (1982). On exports and economic growth. *Journal of Development Economics,* 12, 59–73.

Grossman, G. and E. Helpman (1991). *Innovation and Growth in the Global Economy,* Cambridge, MA: MIT Press.

Helpman, E. and P. Krugman (1989). *Trade Policy and Market Structure,* Cambridge, MA: MIT Press.

Klein, L.R. (2004). New growth centres in this globalized economy. *Journal of Policy Modelling,* 26(4), 499–505.

Leamer, E. (1988). Measures of openness. In *Trade Policy and Empirical Analysis*, R. Baldwin (Ed.), Chicago: Chicago University Press.

Letiche, J.M. (2006). Positive economic incentives, new behavioural economics and successful economic transition. *Journal of Asian Economics*, 17(5), 775–796.

Michaelopoulos, C (1999). Trade Policy and Market Access Issues for Developing Countries. World Bank PRWP No. 2214.

Panagariya, A. (2004). Miracles and debacles: in defence of trade openness. *The World Economy*, 27(8), 1149–1171.

Rodriguez, F. and D. Rodrik (1999). Trade policy and economic growth: A skeptic's guide to cross-national evidence. NBER Working Paper No. W7081.

Sachs, J. and A. Warner (1995). Economic reform and the process of global integration, Brookings Papers on Economic Activity, 1, 1–118.

Stiglitz, J. (2002). *Globalization and Its Discontents*, W.W. Norton & Company.

Summers, R., A. Heston and B. Aten (2001). Penn World Table Version 6.0. Center for International Comparisons at the University of Pennsylvania (CICUP).

Thirlwall, A.P. (2000). Trade, trade liberalisation and economic growth: Theory and evidence, pp. 1–27 Economic Research Paper No. 63, African Development Bank.

Thirlwall, A.P. and Hussain, N.M. (1982). The balance of payments constraint, capital flows and economic growth rate differences between developing countries. *Oxford Economic Papers*, 34(3), 498–509.

United Nations (2003). Liberalisation and Globalisation: The Issues at Stake for the South and for UNCTAD, pp. 1–60, Geneva, Switzerland; South Centre, United Nations.

UNCTAD (2001). Trade Analysis and Information System, CD ROM, Version 8.0. Geneva, Switzerland: United Nations.

UNCTAD (2004). *Handbook of Statistics*. Geneva, Switzerland: United Nations.

UNCTAD (2006). Trade and Development Report, 2006. Geneva, Switzerland: United Nations.

Wacziarg, R. and K.H. Welch (2003). Trade Liberalisation and Growth: New Evidence. pp. 1–75, Working Paper No. 10152, National Bureau of Economic Research, Cambridge, MA.

Winters, L.A. (2004).Trade liberalisation and economic performance: An overview, *Economic Journal,* 114(493), F4–F21.

Wolf, M. (2004). *Why Globalisation Works,* Connecticut, USA: Yale University Press.

World Bank (1987). World Bank Development Report 1987, Washington, DC.

World Bank (1993). *The East Asian Miracle: Economic Growth and Public Policy.*

Washington, DC: World Bank Policy Research Report.

World Bank (2000). International Trade and Development: Data on Import Tariff and NTBs, Washington, DC.

2

SERVICES UNDER WTO—A FRAMEWORK BENEFITS AND CONCERNS FOR INDIA

Prof. Prahlad Kumar & Miss Pramita Srivastava***

GATS—The General Agreement on Trade in Services (GATS) came into existence as a result of the Uruguay Round of negotiations and entered into force on 1 January 1995, with establishment of the WTO.

The Multilateral legal instruments resulting from the Uruguay Round were treated as a single undertaking, India also signed ail the WTO agreement under the single undertaking Rule and GATS is part of this whole package. Prior to the Uruguay Round, services were considered to offer less potential for trade expansion than goods, thanks to existence of technical, institutional and regulatory barriers. However, the development of new transmission technologies have facilitated the supply of services (e.g. satellite communication, electronic banking, tele-education), the opening of monopolies in many countries (e.g. voice telephony), and gradual liberalization of hitherto regulated sectors like transport, banking and insurance combined with

* Professor & Dy. Coordinator, SAP-II, Department of Economics, University of Allahabad, Allahabad.

** Research Scholar, Department of Economics, University of Allahabad, Allahabad.

changes in consumer preference and enhanced the "tradability" of services.

These developments increased international services flows and created a similar need for multilateral disciplines—as in the area of goods.

Thus the main purpose for the creation of the GATS was to create a credible and reliable system of international trade rules, which ensured fair and equitable treatment of all countries on the principles of non-discrimination. It aims at stimulating trade and development by seeking to create a predictable policy environment where in the member countries voluntarily undertake to bind their policy regimes relating to trade in services.

The GATS covers all internationally traded services with two exceptions: services provided to the public in the exercise of governmental authority, and in the air transport sector, traffic rights and all services directly related to the exercise of traffic rights. The WTO secretariat has divided all services into the following twelve sectors:

1. *Business services:* Professional, Computer and related Services, Research and Development Services, Real Estate Services, Rental/Leasing Services without operators and Other Business Services.
2. *Communication Services:* Postal Services, Courier Services, Tele-Communication Services, Audiovisual Services and Other.
3. *Construction and Engineering services:* General construction work for buildings, General construction work for civil engineering, Installation and assembly work, Building completion and finishing work and Other.
4. *Distribution Services:* Commission agents; Wholesale and retail trade Franchising, Retailing Services and Other.
5. *Educational Services:* Primary education services, Secondary education services, Higher education services, Adult education and other education services.
6. *Environmental Services:* Sewage services, Refuse disposal services, Sanitation and similar services and Other.

7. *Financial Services:* All insurance and insurance-related services, Banking and other financial services and Other.
8. *Health Related and Social Services:* Hospital services, other Human Health Services, Social services and Other.
9. *Tourism and Travel Related Services:* Hotels and restaurants, Travel agencies and tour operators services, Tourist guides services and other.
10. *Recreational, Cultural and Sporting Services:* Entertainment services, News agency services, Libraries, archives, museums and other cultural services, Sporting and other recreational services and other.
11. *Transport Services:* Maritime transport services, Internal Waterways Transport, Air Transport Services, Space Transport, Rail Transport Services, Road Transport Services, Pipeline Transport, Services auxiliary to all modes of transport and Other Transport Services.
12. *Other Services:* Not Elsewhere Classified

These twelve areas are further divided into 161 sub-sectors.

Obligations contained in GATS may be categorized into two groups—

(a) General obligations
(b) Conditional Obligations.

(a) General Obligations

General Obligations applies directly and automatically to all member countries of the WTO, regardless of the existence of commitments made for each other The general obligations includes:—

(i) Most Favoured Nation (MFN) Treatment Favour one favours all. MFN means treating one's trading partners equally under GATS. If a country allows foreign competition in a sector, equal opportunities in that sector should be given to service providers from all other WTO members (This applies even if the country has made no specific commitment to provide foreign companies access to its markets under WTO).

(ii) *Transparency:* Member countries are required *inter alia,* to publish all members of general applications and establish national enquiry points to respond to other members information requests.

(iii) *Other unconditional obligations:* include the establishment of administrative review at appeals, procedures and disciplines on the operation of monopolies and exclusive suppliers.

(b) Conditional Obligations

GATS follows a positive list of approach under which each member is expected to undertake specific liberalization commitments through a process called "scheduling". Each member identifies the service sectors/sub-sectors and modes of supply in which it is willing to make commitments. Then the member inscribes the conditions under which it will allow services and service supplier's access to its market. Including limitations does this. It wishes to place on market access and national treatment while granting access. *Thus, national treatment is not mandatory in GATS but is negotiated on a sector-to-sector basis.*

This contrasts with the way the national treatment principle is applied to goods—in that case, once a product has crossed a border and been cleared by the customs it has to be given national treatment even if the importing countries has not made any commitment under the WTO to bind the tariff rate.

(i) **Market Access:-** The granting of market access is a commitment undertaken by individual members in specified sectors after negotiations. It may be made subject to one or more limitations. For example, limitations may be improved on the number of services suppliers, services operations or employees in a sector, the value of transactions, the legal form of the service supplier, or the extent of participation of foreign capital.

(ii) **National Treatment:-** National treatment means treating one's own national and foreigners equally. In services, it means that once a foreign company has been allowed to supply a service in one's country there should be no discrimination between the foreign and local companies.

Under GATS, a country only has to apply this principle when it has made a specific commitment to provide foreigners access to apply national treatment in sectors where it has not made any commitment even though the service is permitted under liberalized regime. Even in the sectors where it has made commitment for market access, GATS does allow limitations on national treatment to be taken fully or partially.

Modes of Supply of Services:

GATS Provides Four Modes of Supply of Services—

Mode 1: Cross-border trade

Mode 2: Consumption abroad.

Mode 3: Commercial Presence.

Mode 4: Presence & movement of natural persons.

Mode 1

Cross-border trade corresponds with the normal form of trade in goods and maintains a clear geographical separation between seller and buyer. In this case, services flow from the territory of another member crossing national frontiers, (e.g. Banking or architectural services transmitted via telecommunications or mail).

Mode 2

Consumption abroad refers to situations where a service consumer moves into another member's territory to obtain a service (e.g. Consumer travelling for tourism, medical treatment, to attend educational establishment).

Mode 3

Commercial presence is the supply of a service through the commercial presence of the foreign supplier in the territory of another WTO member, in this case, a service supplier of one member establishes a territorial presence, including through ownership or leave of premises, in another member's territory to provide a service, (e.g. the establishment of branch office or agencies to deliver such services as banking, legal advice or communications).

Mode 4

Presence of natural persons involves the admission of foreign national to another country to provide service there. An annex to the GATS *makes it clear, however that the agreement has nothing to do with individuals looking for employment in another country, or with citizenship, residence, or employment requirements. The members still has a right to regulate the entry and stay of the person concerned, for instance by requiring visas.*

Importance of Services Sector

Broadly defined, a service is a product of human activity aimed to satisfy a human need, which does not constitute a tangible commodity. According to *The Dictionary of Modern Economies* by David W. Pearce (G.Ed.), "they are sometimes referred to as intangible goods; one of their characteristics being that in general they are 'consumed' at the point of production. They are usually non transferable, thus preventing arbitrage in the sense that the service can not be purchased and then resold at a different price." It further adds "in an economic sense, services are any functions or tasks that are performed, for which there is a demand and hence a price determined in the relevant market".

Penguin Dictionary defines services as intangible goods as distinct from physical commodities. The services are difficult to define unambiguously. The output of some services may take physical form (such as a cheque or bank statement), while le money services are consumed at the point of sale, and are not; therefore, transferable (e.g. a concert or a hair cut) service in which knowledge is imparted (e.g., tax consultant/tax-advisor) may be transferable freely from one consumer to another. The intangible nature of much of the output of the service sector creates difficulties in the calculation of unit productivity.

There are many types of services, ranging from heart surgery to road construction, electricity transmission to education, and child care to water purification.

Services are important for employment and employment growth. This is because many traditional services, including distribution education and social services, are labour intensive. Generally speaking, the service sector of the economy is more labour-intensive than the manufacturing sector. But this generalization is misleading because with computerization warehouses, special purpose buildings and other plant and equipment, much of the services sector now employs more capital per worker than manufacturing industry.

The services sector also contributes proportionately less to exports compared with its domestic market than does manufacturing but invisible exports are of growing importance and world trade in service is growing faster than that in physical commodities. Parts of the services sector such as distribution, banking, business services and communication, have been growing very rapidly. The relative faster growth of services compared with other sectors of the economy has ben characteristic of all advanced countries. In the UK, for example the service sector now accounts for about 70% of the national income. The expansion of services has been driven in particular by income-related demand shifts, benefiting for example the hotel and tourist industry, the economic stimulus resulting from new information and communication technologies, and growing importance of basic infrastructure services, including transport, communication and finance, for a wide range of user industries.

Services are coming to dominate the economic activities of countries at virtually every stage of development, making services trade liberalization a necessity for the integration of the world economy. In the high income industrialised economies, the value added by services generally exceeds 60% of total output, for example, 70% in Australia, 71% in France, 60% in Japan, 72% in United States. In many emerging markets, services account for half or more of economic output; 55% in the Czech republic, 59% in Hungary, 54% in Poland. The same applies to many advanced developing or newly industrialised economies, such as Argentina, Brazil, Korea, Malaysia, Mexico and Thailand.

In many developing economies as well, the service sector is the single largest contributor to economic output, ahead of either agriculture or industry. Even allowing for the fact that governments are major service providers (education, healthcare, sanitation etc.), the commercial market for services is huge and growing in virtually every country. And the trend is clear: as national economics develop and income rise, the commercial service sector accounts for an ever-larger share of GDP.

If we look at the contribution of different sectors to GDP growth in India since 1950-51 to 2000-01, we observe that the growth rate of the service sector during 80's was 6.6% while it became still higher to 7.6% during 90's. This growth rate in 90's was higher than in agriculture and even industry sector. We observe a similar experience of growing contribution of services sector to GDP in many other developing countries of the world. It is, however, not yet clear whether it is the comparative advantage that is driving up the share of the services sector in GDP or whether the services sector in GDP or whether the sector also derives strength from the policy that are being pursued since the early 90's.

The growing importance of services such in the Indian economy can also be looked from the angle of employment, where as services sector accounted for 18.1% of the total employment during 1965-66, it is growing gradually to become 23.5% of the total employment during 1999-2000.

Table 1. Sector-wise Average Shares, Growth Rates and Contribution to GDP Growth (%)

Period	*Agriculture*			*Industry#*			*Services*		
	Share in GDP	*Growth Rate*	*Contribution to GDP*	*Share in GDP*	*Growth Rate*	*Contribution to GDP*	*Share in GDP*	*Growth Rate*	*Contribution to GDP*
1950-51 to 1959-60*	56	2.3	42.5	16.0	5.7	25.3	28.2	4.1	32.2
1960-61 to 1969-70	47.8	2.5	29.2	21.1	6.5	32.9	31.4	4.9	38.1
1970-71 to 1979-80	42.8	1.3	18.6	22.8	3.7	28.7	34.4	4.5	52.7
1980-81 to 1989-90	36.4	4.4	27.5	25.0	6.8	28.9	38.6	6.6	43.0

1990-91 to 2000-2001	28.6	2.9	14.8	27.1	5.9	27.6	44,3	7.6	57.6

#- inclusive of construction

* nine year data for growth and weighted contribution since data for 1949-50 are not available. Due to rounding off, sectoral data may not add up to 100.

Source: National Accounts Statistics, CSO.

Table 2. Share of Services Sector in Total Employment

Period	*Employment in Services Sector (in crore)*	*Total Employment (in crore)*	*Share of Services in Total Employment*
1965-66	3.97	21.93	18.1
1970-71	4.2	24.09	20.0
1980-81	5.71	30.24	18.9
1990-91	8.70	35.68	24.4
1999-2000	10.29	43.81	23.5

Source: National Sample Survey Organization (various rounds) and Visaria, 1996. RBI Report on Currency and Finance 2000-01.

According to Pramit Bhaduri, Increase in the share of services in employment could imply a growth of low productivity, low income informal sector. However, if the increase in earnings per worker in the services sector is higher than with the industry it could mean that part of the increase in employment in the services sector is in the formal/ organized sector, may be public sector, or in the new IT related industries with higher use of capital worker.

Freer trade in services enables countries to better enjoy the benefits of globalization and improves economic efficiency just as freer trade in goods does. It contributes to job creation, higher incomes, more consumer choice, downward pressure on inflation and a better quality of life.

Liberalizations of trade in services is an important means to encourage the continued rapid expansion of foreign direct investment, to integrate national economies more effectively and to reduce income and other disparities among countries. Because services production and consumption normally are proximate and simultaneous, services trade usually entails a significant transfer of technology and know-how from country to country. This is critical especially for developing and emerging markets, which can acquire state-of-the- art skills relatively quickly and inexpensively through time and expense that would be required to develop them denovo.

Global Trends in Services Sector

The importance of services sector can be judged from the fact that world trade in commercial services amounted to US $ 1440 billion in the year 2001, which is 23% of goods trade. In India too, services accounted for 49% of GDP in 2000-01 while agriculture accounted for 27% of GDP and manufacturing 23%.

Throughout the 1999-2000, amongst the leading traders in commercial services the most dynamic with exports and imports growing at double-digit rates were China, the Republic of Korea, India, Ireland and Malaysia.

Table 3. Some of the Leading Exporters of Commercial Services, 2001
(Billion dollars and percentage)

Exporters	*Value*	*Share*	*Annual Percentage Change*		
			1990-2000	*2000*	*2001*
United States	262.9	18.3	7	9	-3
United Kingdom	108.5	7.5	8	3	-6
Germany	79.8	5.5	5	-3	-1
France	79.0	5.5	2	-1	-3
Japan	63.3	4.4	5	13	-7
Hong Kong,	43.0	3.0	9	13	2
China	34.7	2.4	7	7	-5
Canada	32.0	2.2	18	15	3
China	28.4	2.0	12	12	-2
Korea, Rep of	20.1	1.4	14	26	14
India	19.2	1.3	18	8	15
Ireland	13.6	.9	14	15	0
Malaysia	1440.0	100.0	6	6	-1
World					

Source: Annual Report, 2002, World Trade Organisation.

Table 4. Some of the Leading Importers of Commercial Services, 2001 (Billion dollars and percentage)

Exporters	*Value*	*Share*	*Annual Percentage Change*		
			1990-2000	*2000*	*2001*
United States	187.6	18.1	7	16	-7
United Kingdom	88.5	6.2	8	2	-5
Germany	128.5	9.0	5	-3	-3
France	60.0	4.2	2	-3	_2
Japan	106.7	7.5	3	1	-8
Canada	39.6	2.8	4	7	-4
China	36.4	2.5	24	16	2
Korea, Rep. of	32.6	2.3	13	23	-1
India	23.7	1.7	13	15	21
Ireland	33.6	2.4	19	8	17
Malaysia	16.3	1.1	12	13	-2
World	1430.0	100.0	6	6	-1

Source: Annual Report, 2002, World Trade Organization.

The impact of the slowdown in commercial services trade differed largely among the major regions. Most of them including Asia, reported decline in export and import in 2001. The down turn in the Asian region was particularly pronounced for Japan. However, China, Hong-Kong and India recorded a higher commercial services export receipts in 2001 with an annuals growth rate of 3%, 2% and 14% respectively. India's growth performance in the world services trade is remarkable considering the fact that during the decade 1999-2000 and in 2001 there are only a few countries, which have registered a double-digit growth. .

Among the Asian leading, India features sixth in the list of exporters and fourth in the list of importers in these of terms in 2001 but what is noteworthy is that India is reached first when annual percentage change for 2001 is considered.

Domestic Services Sector

Services trade has undergone considerable growth in India. When we see the latest export and import figures of commercial services in India in the above tables, this fact becomes more evident. Software and services are seen as India's really big competitive advantage while exports of IT and IT-enabled services have gone up from $ 1.8 billion in 1997-98 to $ 9.9 billion in 2003-04.

We also observe that services exports from India grew at around 17% per annum during 1990s, which was about three times the global average for services exports. In 2000, India's export of services including software, were $18.3 billion. The software exports comprised around 30% of services exports, other major services exported include travel (17%), transportations (10%) and financial services, management consulting, even construction (4%).

Table 5. Exports of Services ($ billion)

	1997-98	*1998-99*	*1999-2000*	*2000-01*	*2001-02*
Services of which,	9.43	13.19	15.71	18.87	20.29
Software	1.76	2.63	4.02	6.34	7.18
Communication	0.17	0.60	1.06	1.29	0.92
Travel	2.91	2.99	3.04	3.17	2.91
Transportations	1.84	1.93	1.71	1.19	1.97

Source: RBI Bulletin, May 2003.

India offers a large pool of services and all the modes of supply of services are important to the country. The emergence of information technology opens up the possibility of cross-border trade (i.e. mode 1) and India 's natural endowment makes it an attractive destination for tourists, which is trade through consumption abroad (i.e. Mode 2). However, since India's core strength lies in the quality of its professionals from reputed institutes, it is mode 4, which is most important. It is only to be expected that India seek greater market access in mode 4 while at the same time also ensures greater FDI flow into the country.

Where Are We in Services Negotiations

According to Jalan (Bimal), "Services revolution" which is one of the characteristics of globalisation—presents unprecedented opportunities for India. This has been facilitated by unprecedented and unforeseen advances in computer and communication technology. As a result, the development of certain services is now regarded as one of the preconditions of economic growth and not as one of its consequences. Another important aspect of the 'services revolution' is that geography and levels of industrialisation are no longer the primary determinants of the location of facilities for production of services.

Jalan noted that the fastest growing segment of services is the rapid expansion of knowledge-based services such as professional, technical services. India has a tremendous advantage in the supply of such services because of a developed structure of technological and educational institutions, such as this one, and lower labour costs.

> "The primary source of comparative advantage today are: skills and ability to adopt and change. And, India has the advantage of skills, of entrepreneurship and of managerial competence in taking advantage of these changes."

India's main objective in the negotiations in trade in services is to induce our trading partners to undertake more liberal commitments in cross-border supply of services (Mode I) and movement of natural persons (Mode IV). Cross-border supply of services, especially through electronic mode of delivery, is an area of key interest to us. With regard to movement of natural persons, India and other developing countries have taken up a number of related issues, such as recognition of qualifications, economic need tests (ENTs), administrative procedures relating to visas, mutual recognition agreements (MRAs), and social security contributions. While India's main interest is in liberalization of Mode 1 and Mode 4, the core interest of most of our trading partners is in Mode 3 (commercial presence), with request either to bind the presently applicable FDI policy or to offer a more liberal policy.

India submitted its initial offer in Dec 2003 for specific commitments to 62 member countries. It had received initial requests from 27 member countries in various service sectors. As many as 48 member countries have submitted their initial offer as of now. Through the initial conditional offer, the existing Uruguay Round Commitments in sectors such as engineering services, computer and related services, financial services, health services, tourism services have been improved, fresh commitments in new sectors such as accounting and bookkeeping services, medical and dental services, services provided by midwives, nurses, physiotherapists and para-medical personnel and maritime transport services, have also been offered.

India is currently engaged in bilateral discussion with trading partners on our initial conditional offers and also on the response to India's request, particularly in Modes 1 and 4, in the initial offers tabled by our trading partners.

Acknowledgement

An earlier draft of the paper was presented in a National Seminar on "WTO and Indian Economy", organised by the Department of Economics, University of Allahabad, Allahabad from April 23 to 24, 2005. We acknowledge it with thanks.

REFERENCES

* Jalan, Bimal (2002), "India and the Challenge of Globalisation", *The Indian Economic Journal*, Jan.-March, 2001-2002, Vol. 49, No. 3.
* Jain, Sunil (2003), "Who's Afraid of Free Trade", *Margin*, Oct.-Dec., 2003, Vol. 36, No. 1.
* Kapila, Uma (eds.) "Growth and Structural Change since 1950", *Indian Economy Since Independence*, 3rd edition; Academic Foundation, Daryaganj, New Delhi.
* Government of India, Ministry of Finance; Economic Survey-2004-05.
* http://: commerce, nic.in
* http://: dgft.delhi nic.in
* www.ficci.com
* www.iimb.ernet.in
* www. oecsd.org

3

WTO—DOES IT REPRESENT A NEW PERSPECTIVE TO DEVELOPMENT?

*Smriti Mukherjee**

After the end of the Second World War, of the three new institutions namely IMF, World Bank and the GATT that were set up the last one was probably the weakest. While the IMF was entrusted with the task of looking after short run balance of payment needs World Bank concentrated itself with long term development finance. GATT tried to expand world trade by emphasizing mainly on tariff cutting devices. Although based on the sound principles of most favoured nation treatment, non discrimination, reciprocity and national treatment tariff cutting procedures adopted in different GATT rounds of discussion occupied the centre stage of attention. In order to infuse new lease of life to this organization WTO was created so that the link between trade and other sectors of mi economy becomes prominent Reduction in tariff rate is important for expanding trade no doubt but new issues were emerging which GATT was expected to handle in an efficient manner. In order to achieve this objective some organizational changes were necessary and that is why GATT was converted into WTO.

In the present paper we would like to concentrate on the following three issues: what are the new measures adopted to expand trade, whether this has changed the perspective on development altogether and if this necessarily involves a conflict between developed and developing countries.

* Gokhale Institute of Politics and Economics, Pune.

I

New market access was sought to be created by progressive reduction in tariffs. Harbinson progressive reduction formula aimed at a reduction rate of 35% if tariffs were below 15 percent, 60% for tariffs within the 15-90 per pent limit and 65% for tariffs above 90% limit in the case of developed countries. For developing countries three inflexion points for tariff levels at 20, 60 and 120 per cent were selected the rates of reduction for which were placed at 20, 30,40 and 45 per cent. Reduction in tariff rates brought down domestic distortion and increased competitive power of exports of the home country since tariff reduction was a global phenomenon. The additional market access created by the WTO was expected to result in larger export revenue. Higher profitability in export sector would attract more resources into it ensuring better allocation of resources. Cheaper imports would make quality imports possible which will ultimately raise the standards of export production.

Reduction in tariff rate would alter domestic macroeconomic scene in several ways. Greater product variety is a distinct possibility owing to increased competition. New people join the labour force as a result of which household income increases. Consumption standard rises along with new types of goods being incorporated in the consumption basket. If the growth propelling industries happen to be located in the urban areas people will migrate from rural to urban areas leading to a downward pressure on wages. Once the process of liberalization proceeds further newer industries will be set up creating more demand for skilled labour, since we assume that more complex types of industries will come up with development. Skilled unskilled wage divide would increase but average wage rate might increase as well.

Increase in employment will in all probability be accompanied by rise in per capita income which in its turn might stimulate the saving rate. Higher saving might easily get transformed into higher investment rate which leads to an overall higher growth rate for the economy. In case suitable investment outlets are not forthcoming there would be an excess of saving over investment leading to a decrease in aggregate demand. If however capital account liberalization is also there surplus resources might generate an outward flow of funds which means that the economy concerned emerges as a net lender to the rest of the world. This result of course depends upon the assumption that net export earnings contribute a respectable share of gross domestic product. In order to take full advantage of increased market access range of products to be offered to the world market has to be substantially augmented.

Globalization offers a unique opportunity for technological innovation also. If an economy had been operating inside the production possibility frontier production of new items would push it to the boundaries of the frontier. Fuller utilization of resources would make production system more efficient and convergence in growth rate throughout the world might become a reality. Developing countries can add to the product range mainly through imitation. As knowledge and information travel faster imitation lag reduces and developing countries might offer stiff competition. Emergence of new products definitely points towards technological innovation and it can be verified by undertaking a physical counting of products. The other channel of technological innovation namely research and development activity will be more prominent in the developed regions of the world. Rate of innovation made possible by creating new product range might exceed the rate that results from increased spending on research and development In that case difference in growth rate as between developed and developing countries will be narrowed down.

It is quite possible that in order to attain technological maturity R and D expenditure has to be substantially stepped up on the part of developing countries. Only imitation is not enough, a substantial increase in R and D expenditure has the capability to push the production frontier to the right. Raising of funds to finance the R and D expenditure is an important issue in the case of developing countries but the mode of financing is important as well. If a firm, whether private or public, raises resources internally to finance R and D expenditure it is the most desirable thing and that firm is termed as a productive sector. Here research activity is an internal affair in the sense that financial provision to carry on research is arranged internally. To give a rightward push to the production possibility frontier a critical minimum effort may be necessary which means a deviation from the standard path of routine R and D expenditure. Total factor productivity growth is a direct concomitant of successful R and D expenditure. Over active research department or wasteful expenditure on research would be manifested in lower total factor productivity growth and lower accumulation of R and D.

While it is true that globalization provides a positive impetus towards technological innovation adoption of new techniques entails some additional expenditure which is not strictly financial. For instance a higher education level on an average makes the learning process much easier and entails lesser burden on the firm to undertake technological innovation. Similarly a sound system of intellectual property rights is expected to provide encouragement to research and development. Rate of return on R and D is another determinant of higher research expenditures on the part of competing firms. Therefore to take foil advantage of the opportunities provided by globalization it is not only the internal organization of firms but over all macroeconomic set up of the developing counties might have to be altered.

Restriction on agricultural subsidies represents another area for expansion of trade on the part of developing countries. Both U.S.A. and European Union are quite protective towards their agriculture. Common agricultural policies and sliding scale duties practised by EU nations are known throughout the world. WTO directive regarding scaling down of duties would bring out the comparative advantage of developing country agricultural exports. Low cost agricultural production by the developing countries could not find markets owing to competitive pressure exerted by the developed countries. They maintained competitive strength by fiscal measures. Once these incentives are removed one stumbling block in the way of international trade would definitely be removed. But if one has to evaluate relative strength of trade creating effects released by reduction of tariffs and subsidies it is likely to be more in the case of the former. This is because cut in agricultural subsidies creates a larger market no doubt but differences in product quality happen to be an impediment to trade. For instance butter, cheese or other dairy products are produced in developing countries also but they may not be of exportable quality in the world market. Machine made items are standardized and so chances of attaining uniform quality are more compared to those in the case of agriculture based items. Problems regarding preservation, maintaining hygienic standards etc present important problems which are to be overcome if agricultural exports are to succeed.

II

A New Perspective on Development?

When GATT was set up in the year 1948 it was looked upon as an institution laying down the basic rules governing international trade. GATT rounds of discussion held after a gap of every four or five years were utilized as tariff cutting exercise on manufactured goods. Since everything was on reciprocal basis, initiative on the part of developing countries to come prepared with requests of tariff reduction on certain selected items was quite difficult because an offer list of tariff reduction on their part was also mandatory. Request list and offer list of tariff reduction were to be presented simultaneously when discussions were taking place. Although as a philosophy it was all right in the sense that no concession to developing countries was involved, everybody was treated at par, still the question remained regarding unequal economic status. A set of countries were entitled to offer tariff cuts but whether it would be of any value to the countries negotiating the offer was an open question.

To give a push to the widening of markets what was necessary was a unilateral step towards tariff reduction on an aggregative basis. Instead of the commodity by commodity approach or grouping of commodities and then applying across the board reduction a new concept of increased market access was put on the agenda. While reduction of tariff rates on the part of developed countries would expand the horizon of the market developing countries would find it easier to buy things from the world market since no duties were to be paid subsequently to the home country government. Comparison of home price with world market price would help them find out where true comparative advantage is and developing countries will accordingly decide to specialize. Many of the things they were producing at home under tariff protection would probably be given up in favour of straight away imports from the foreign countries.

This approach towards development was in sharp contradiction to the import substituting strategy of industrialization followed by majority of the developing countries during the post war period. Urge to attain self sufficiency, export pessimism and conserving foreign exchange were some of the leading considerations behind choice of import substitution strategy. And it was more or less okayed by the developed countries in the expectation that the new industrial plants to be set up would vitally depend upon supplies from the west and the USA. Country tied or project tied aid that was to be provided ensured that developed country savings would not be wasted, they would find better outlets. In addition to these economic considerations the political necessity of wining over developing countries and take them to the sides of super powers was very strong indeed. Various models linking import substitution to economic growth (Chenery model, for instance) were prepared which shows that theoretical support was also not lacking.

Import substituting industrialization created several problems in the way of smooth functioning of markets. To protect the newly set up industries high rate of protection was necessary since their average cost of production was higher owing to limited quantity of production. To ensure sale of domestically produced goods an elaborate system of import licensing was necessary. In India the twin principles of licensing were said to be essentiality and indigenous non-availability. It was to some extent save the foreign exchange expenditure on imports as well. Introduction of physical restriction on imports in the form of quotas and state trading in selected commodities constituted other facets of import trade control policy. Maintenance of strict pegging rate system required frequent intervention by the central bank making it impossible for market forces to operate. Pegged rate system gave rise to black market transaction involving foreign currency because there was always suppressed excess demand. Import licenses were sold at a premium and managing one license meant fairly large amount of windfall. Rigidity of exchange rate coupled with rising inflation rate made over valuation of currency a frequent phenomenon.

Starting from the late sixties many countries made a turn around from import substitution to export promotion. India was also one of them but the attempt was halfhearted. It lost steam over the years and another start was made during Rajiv Gandhi era. It finally culminated in the full fledged liberalization policy adopted since 1991. This shift in trade policy from local to globally determined policy initiatives marked a complete reversal of the earlier policy being followed. Giving a free play to market forces meant distortions were to disappear to a large extent. Establishment of current account convertibility, near total abolition of import licensing system, liberalization of capital account transactions and export led growth in general contributed to a paradigm shift in trade policy for the world as a whole. And the most note worthy thing about this change is that it was exogenous. Policy of globalization and liberalization was formulated under the auspices of the IMF and the World Bank and WTO as an organization decided not to oppose it. Thus trade policy came to be determined not under the influence of national priorities but compulsion of international policy coordination. Synchronization of policy initiatives in the sphere of trade policy was supposed to minimize frictions.

Increased emphasis on trade and renewed faith in trade acting as an engine of growth signified a change in development policy in one important way. During fifties, sixties and to a lesser extent during seventies also official development assistance played a significant role in development policies chosen by the third world. Activities relating to agriculture, industry, infrastructure and social services received large quantities of development aid to bridge the gap in financing. Because foreign exchange resources mobilized through exports were inadequate to meet import needs bilateral or multilateral aid were offered in plenty to fill in the gap. The oil crisis during seventies and the debt crisis during early eighties that struck the world made it clear that the amount of resources that would be required to bailout the economies involved would be well beyond the capacities of multilateral aid. Monterry Conference which was held much later supported this approach of reduced dependence on aid as a source of development financing. The countries which were in urgent need of funds would get priority in the matter of aid allocation. For the remaining countries trade was singled out as the most important source of foreign exchange earner. Foreign private capital emerged to be another significant component of development finance. Since commodity prices and exchange rate were to be market determined it was but natural that external saving would be routed through market channel. Government intervention whether in the matter of trade or aid was kept to the minimum.

Tariff binding is another novel instrument that was attempted during the Uruguay discussions. Previously national governments were free to raise export and import duties on their own. Binding of tariff rates made the upper limit on tariffs quite sticky. Once a country committed itself to the bound rate it became fixed and it could not be altered under any fiscal compulsion. This innovation injected an element of certainty in the sphere of international trade because foreign producers could know beforehand how much of duty they had to pay and whether any cost cutting is necessary to maintain competitiveness. Maximum permissible rate of tariffs was determined from outside and it ensured uniformity in the matter of rate fixation. Individual countries enjoyed leverage when their actual tariff rates were below the bound rates. They could easily increase it without violating international provision. Looked at another way there was no need for the countries to lower their tariff rate it it were below the actual bound rate agreed upon at the WTO.

In order to do justice to the debate as to whether WTO propagates a different outlook towards development issues one needs to take up the issues relating to respective roles of state and market in economic development. During the fifties and sixties planning as looked upon as the only answer to economic development of backward countries and therefore an interventionist state was accepted as a fait accompli. There were frequent market failures resulting in rate of inflation higher than the rest of the world rate, over valuation of exchange rate, poor efficiency of governance etc. Too much of restrictions throttled individual initiative as a result of which government was forced to undertake many activities which are strictly essential for a government.

An attitude of neo-liberalism swept through the entire world in the aftermath of debt crisis. It was a sort of counter revolution when full freedom to market forces was advocated as a solution to inefficiencies in various spheres of the economy. Instead of being viewed as market failures these temporary breakdowns were looked upon as government failures and hence privatization came to be projected as a solution to the normal ills affecting an economy. Thus mergers, acquisitions and disinvestment by public sector units came to be regarded as being the order of the day. Better allocation of resources leading to more efficiency in production was cited to be the chief feature of this new development strategy.

The adjustment to the new strategy was not without its pains. Increase in unemployment, more misery to the small farmer and higher incidence of poverty were some of the problems brought about by the new strategy. Of the three problems mentioned by us the last one was probably not directly connected with WTO, it was more due to the structural adjustment policy followed simultaneously with trade liberalization. Structural adjustment policy that was to address long run equilibrium needs of the economic system aimed at balancing of budget through reduction of subsidies. Abolition of food subsidies led to disappearance of public distribution system in many places accentuating magnitude of poverty. Similarly acute distress suffered by farmers led to higher incidence of suicides in many poverty stricken areas. All these disturbing developments led to rethinking on the part of IMF and the World Bank and modifications were suggested so that the transition from the old to the new policy calls for lesser sacrifice.

The amendments that were suggested basically centred around the role of government. Unless proper infrastructures are provided by the government markets cannot function.

Thus a sound legal framework defending intellectual property rights was found necessary in case a country wanted to attract FDI. To protect the domestic producers from unfair trading practices like dumping anti dumping laws and a vigilant body to detect cases of dumping are necessary. While discussing subsidy issues food security aspect got the priority from World Bank and IMF also came up with safety nets provision. Targeted rationing instead of rationed food for everybody was advocated. Good governance in general was seen as a basic constituent for the success of this new policy. Public sector was not expected to interfere with the market but provide the supporting devices so that markets are enabled to function effectively and efficiently. Currently the policy that is being followed throughout the world makes it a distinct exercise in the sense that although liberalization is being favoured it is not the same thing as mercantilist policy of laissez faire.

Another basic trait of development policy that emerged since the discussion of Washington Consensus relates to the concept of monitored development. Instead of each nation fixing its own development agenda based on some doctrine like balanced growth or unbalanced growth a common approach was suggested to tackle the long run economic issues. It moved away from Keynes, Harrod-Domar or Nurkse where broad macroeconomic issues occupied the core areas of development. The present approach focuses more on micro foundation of Macroeconomics. Thus decision making power of women within a given household, micro credit societies and self help groups started by women and their impact on rural economy are getting lot of attention. Many studies dealing with market efficiency under WTO show that in the name of standardization many women doing order supplying business in the textile industry are being gradually eased out. Household or more precisely gender issues are being discussed more openly in connection with development.

We have referred to the Washington Consensus. But two other important developments in the area relate to Millennium Development Goals and Monterry Conference. Gender issues and more focused development agenda constituted the focus of these two international events. More representation to women, elimination of gender gap in the sphere of higher education are declared to be avowed objectives of Millennium Development Goals. The Monterry Conference asked for more rights on the part of donor countries to choose the beneficiary as well the project. It is further away from the heydays of UNCTAD when developed countries had to agree to donate at least one percent of their GDP for the poor countries. Instead of any such dictum aid giving nations are asking for more freedom in the matters of selection of aid receiving countries and the new financial instruments which can be utilized to distribute aid. Percolation approach to development or for that matter targeted approach also are discarded. What we get as the end result is that macro issues are being discussed at the micro level. Given this broad policy environment WTO has to follow a conformist approach to development.

III

Who Benefits and How?

The declared objectives of GATT made it clear that it was an organization which was strictly concerned with growth of free trade. In the process it did not distinguish between rich and poor nations and so hardly any concession was shown to the developing countries. Still there was a clause that pertained to the developing countries and it was known as special and differential treatment. Ordinarily GATT would not allow any quantitative restriction on trade. However given that a particular developing country had acute balance of payment problem quotas were temporarily permitted. This was an instance where special consideration was shown to the needs of developing areas. To some extent this provision helped IMF because freedom to impose quotas lessened the burden of providing short run accommodation to the poor countries with BOP deficit. Without asking for financial assistance from the IMF developing countries could reduce trade deficit on their own by taking recourse to quotas.

The second instance of sympathetic treatment arose when developing countries were permitted to seek tariff reduction without at the same time indicating the items on which they could announce tariff reduction Trade negotiations were carried out on strictly give and take basis which were termed as reciprocal approach. When two groups of developed countries were bargaining over tariff reduction on certain commodities the outcome of the agreement applied automatically to poorer nations.

Barring these small concessions GATT was able to maintain its impartial nature over the years. The fact that much remained to be done for the developing countries if there were to be a fair distribution of the gains from trade is evident from the fact that a separate institution called UNCTAD had to be set up in the year 1964. That is still there but setting up of WTO has largely implied a shift in the centre of activity. The successive Ministerial meetings have generated much interest in international trade circles about the future course of world trade. One new idea that has emerged in the Doha discussion dwells over the concept of financial compensation to weaker nations that become victim of trade law violations. To illustrate the concept of financial compensation that is still being negotiated one notes that to start with we have to assume some sort of trade violation like dumping or granting of higher subsidies. If the matter is taken to the WTO dispute settlement board it can recommend a tariff escalation against the offending partner.

In principle WTO is committed to a regime of tariff reduction but notwithstanding that tariff escalation provision had to be retained which according to some points towards a possible contradiction in trade policy. That Dispute Settlement Board is empowered to recommend a tariff escalation might have a dampening effect on the spirits of violating nations. The existence of the provision might prevent partner countries to engage into unfair activities. In spite of tariff escalation threat if violations take place the affected country can be partially compensated by improvement in its terms of trade. To incorporate a legal provision of compensation within a given system is a desirable proposition no doubt but the problem arises with regard to developing countries. They do not expect much through tariff retaliation against large countries and the kind of bargaining power that is necessary to effect a reduction in world prices owing to tariff escalation does not exist with them.

It is precisely against this background that the power to grant financial compensation to weaker nations on the part of the Dispute Settlement Board has been mooted. If accepted this would amount to giving power to an international body to impose fine on another sovereign nation. Estimation of the amount of compensation also involves tricky issues in the sense that the injury inflicted upon the affected nation has to be evaluated in money terms. And secondly the aim of the compensation principle has to be settled also. If the financial compensation is calculated in such a way that the affected nation stands on the same welfare level as it was before the violation it may not be fair enough. Taking the case to the Dispute Settlement Board and having the trial and verdict also definitely involve some length of time and the welfare position cannot remain unaffected throughout this interval. Therefore real financial compensation formula should have some element of premium associated with it.

The idea of financial compensation which is yet to receive official approval involves some discriminatory treatment in favour of the poorer countries. But there are areas where policies pursued by the WTO may not be conducive to developing country interests. Market access provision in Agreement on Agriculture may act against the interests of small farmers in poor countries. Lowering of tariffs is likely to result in flooding of markets with quality fruits and vegetables from abroad almost instantly. Small farmers engaged in producing coarse grains or not so standard produce stand to lose out to the foreign competitors. They hardly have the requisite means to compete in the foreign markets and on the top of it they face fierce competition from producers from outside. Loss in farm income may be partially due to decline in market prices resulting from greater availability. Accentuation of poverty is a strong possibility under market access provision.

One way to resist this rural impoverishment is migration to the cities. Provided jobs are available in manufacturing or service sector there may result a downward movement in wages. This downward movement in wages can be arrested only if they are absorbed in the production of exportables or non tradables because lowering of tariffs makes production of importables less attractive and their production will actually decline. If import competing sector is intensive in the use of capital decrease in production will release capital which will be available for employment elsewhere in the economy. Surplus labour from rural areas in combination with capital just being released can give a push to the rightward shift of the production possibility schedule.

Under the impact of globalization and liberalization of service sector this sector may tend to grow at a higher rate. Migrants from rural sector normally will not be able to do the job and demand for skilled workers will rise. Level of education prevailing in the country will largely determine the number of people who can be absorbed in the newly emerging sectors. Wage rate for skilled workers will rise aggravating income inequality within the country. Rural urban wage divide is likely to become sharper until of course outsourcing of job emerges in the economy. When rise in the wage rate also cannot generate sufficient increase in supply of skilled labour immigration rules have to be made more liberal or job outsourcing becomes the reality. Some countries in the Western Europe have already started thinking along the lines of having liberal immigration rules.

Instead of looking upon WTO as a mechanism which is creating rift between rich and poor nations it will be wise to think that it is providing a road to make growth process truly interdependent. To establish the right channels for interdependence an economy needs to set up sound institutions for governance. Legal frame will have to be prepared to lay down rules regarding intellectual property rights, competition laws, rules regarding foreign withdrawal etc. Anti dumping cell will have to be vigilant to guard against unfair trading practices. Growth of right type of institutions is absolutely vital to reap the maximum advantages from being a WTO member.

REFERENCES

1. Anderson, K., Huang, J.J. etc. Long Run Impacts of China's WTO Accession, Policy Research Working Paper 3052, World Bank, May 2003.
2. Anderson, K. and W. Martin, Doha Merchandise Trade Reform, Policy Research Working Paper 3848, World bank, Feb 2006.
3. Andrew, D.F. and M.R. Rosenzweig, Technical Change and Human Capital Returns and Investment, Evidence from the Green Revolution, AER, September 1996, vol 86,no. 4., pp 931-953.
4. Bruno, M., Ravallion, M. etc. Equity and Growth in Developing Countries, Old and New, Policy Research Working Paper l563, World Bank, Jan. 1996.
5. Choudhuri, E., Faruqee and S. Tokarick, Trade Liberalization, Macroeconomic Adjustmentand Welfare, IMF Working Paper WP/06/304, Dec 2006.
6. Frankel, J.A. and D. Romer, Does Trade Cause Growth? AER, June 1999, Vol. 89, No. 3, pp. 379-399.
7. Hertel, T.W., Reimer, J.J. etc. Long Run Impact of China's WTO Accession, Policy Research Working Paper 3052, World Bank, May 2003.
8. lanchovinchina, E. and P. Kacker, Growth Trends in the Developing World, Policy Research Working Paper 3775, World Bank, Nov. 2005,
9. Jean, I. and R. Wacziarg, Stages of Diversification, *AER,* Mar 2003, Vol. 93, No. l, pp. 63-86.
10. Khan, F.A., New Product Technology, Accumulation and Growth, Policy Research Working Paper 3846, World Bank, 2006.
11. Klinger, B., D. Lederman, Diversification, Innovation and Imitation Inside the Global Technological Frontier, Policy Research Working Paper 3872, World Bank, Apr. 2006.
12. Lederman, D. and W.F. Malony, R and D Development, Policy research Working Paper 3024, World Bank, Apr. 2003.
13. Lederman, D. and L. Saenz, Innovation and Development Around the World 1960-2000, Policy Research Working Paper 3774, World Bank, Nov. 2005.
14. Limao, N. and K. Saggi, Tariff Retaliation versus Financial Compensation in the Enforcement of International Trade Agreements, Policy Research Working Paper 3873, World Bank, Apr. 2006.
15. Mattias, L. and L. Sqire, The Simultaneous Evolution of Growth

and Inequality, *The Economic Journal,* 113 (Apr.), 2003, pp. 326-344.

16. Nicita, A. and S. Razzaz, Who Benefits mid How Much?, Policy Research Working Paper 3029, World Bank, Apr. 2003.
17. Nicita, A., Who Benefits From Trade Liberalization in Mexico? Policy Research Working Paper, World Bank, 2004.
18. Nicita, A., Export Led Growth, Pro Poor or Not? Evidence from Madagascar's Textile and Apparel Industry, Policy Research Working Paper 384, World Bank, 2006.
19. Susan, M.C. and B.P. Bosworth, Economic Growth in East Asia: Accumulation vs Assimilation, Brookings Paper on Economic Activity, 1996, 2, pp. 135-204.
20. World Bank, Perspectives on Development, Spring 2005.

4

WTO AND INDIA: OPPORTUNITIES AND CHALLENGES

*Birendra Kumar Jha**

Introduction

The signing of the GATT accord by 120 countries at Marrakesh on the 15th of April, 1994 is possibly the greatest endeavour towards human accord in the second half of the Twentieth Century just as the founding of the United Nations was the greatest achievement of the first half of this century. Thus, establishment of the World Trade Organisation (WTO) which is the embodiment of the result of Uruguay Round held during a long period of about eight years from 1986 to 1994, is possibly a mighty big event in international economic scenario. This new apex body equipped with the legal authority and provisions for enforcing the commitments, rules and norms came into existence on 1st January, 1995. It professes trade liberalisation through an open, rule-based and non-discriminatory multilateral trading system which provides greater trade flows for ail its participating members thereby ensuring fair distribution of the fruits of global economic development. This young institution having 148 countries as its members at present and governing 95% of the global trade emerged as the third economic pillar of worldwide dimension next to the IMF and the IBRD. This biggest international

* Reader & Head, Department of Economics, DBKN College, Narhan, Samastipur, Bihar.

trading organisation helps in implementing the past negotiations, initiating periodic review of the trade policy and settling the trade disputes among its member countries. Evolution of a free trading environment for the movement of goods and services is its objective based on the assumption that free trade is an optimal modality of global welfare. The underlying principles of the WTO are transparency and provision by member of national treatment and most favoured nation treatment to all the members. It is 'the best basis and perhaps the only basis for establishing and maintaining a bilateral world trade order with a system of international legal constraints trade policies under the MFN Principle (WTO Report, 1995).

Need for WTO

Before the WTO was instituted, international trade in merchandise was guided by the rules and provisions of the General Agreement on Tariffs and Trade (GATT). Need for such Agreement was felt in 1947 for reshaping the world economy shattered by the Great Depression (1929-32) and the Second World War (1939-45). Although signatories to GATT have mutually agreed to abide by rules and regulations for orderly international trade, violations of its rules began soon after its inception. The international trade was being conducted in an increasingly protected environment due to the persistent disregard to fair trading practices expected under GATT operations and the ineffective applications of the steps taken at various GATT rounds. Moreover, there were some deficiencies on the part of GATT such as it covered only goods and not trade in services, certain loopholes in the agriculture sector agreements were heavily exploited and efforts at liberalising agricultural trade met with little success and its international structure and dispute settlements were not effective. And so the need felt to undertake negotiations for organising rule-based world trade promoting non-discriminatory multilateral trading system gave birth to the WTO which is a more powerful body having an enlarged role than its predecessors. Of course, the WTO is distinctively as well as qualitatively an improvement over the GATT in many respects such as scope, membership, objectives, functioning and policies. Unlike its predecessor the WTO is a properly established permanent organisation having legal status and enjoying privileges and immunities on the same footing as the IMF and the IBRD.

Cold War

"Never before were a nation borders so open as is happening today with the inception of the WTO" (Mishra, Jagannath, 1997). Undoubtedly, there is greater flow of goods and services among its member countries now than ever before. The first World Trade report reveals the fact that world trade has tripled since 1994 and it forecasts continued increase in future because of opening up of new markets particularly in the developing economics.

Under the dictates of the IMF-World Bank-WTO prescriptions of the LPG strategy as a 'straight jacket solution' for all, a large number of developing countries had to follow such policies. The World Bank has gone to the extent of saying that developing countries which most widely opened their markets to trade in nineties grew three times faster than those which did not. But within very short period the developed countries showed their malafide intention which put the World Bank in surprise. The World Bank expressed its surprise in these words. "It makes no sense for rich countries to encourage developing countries to adopt policies that will promote growth, and then adopt trade policies that reduce the growth progress of these countries". (Global Economic Prospects, 2004: Realising the Promise of the Doha Agenda, published by the World Bank, *Hindustan Times*, Sept. 04, 2003). It is but true that the developed countries are willing to give very little while demanding too much of the developing countries. It is but true that the Quad Countries (USA, EU, Canada, and Japan) with their share of 80% of the global trade dominated the decision-making of WTO. The Annual Report of the World Bank on Global Economic Reform has revealed the truth in these words "There is a stark contrast between words and deeds and double standards applied by the Quad countries (USA, EU, Japan and Canada). The Quad countries tariffs for trade among themselves range from 4.3% in Japan to 8.3% in Canada, but their tariffs to keep out developing country exports are in some cases as high as 550%. Product with high tariffs in Quad countries includes major agricultural stable food products, such as meat, sugar, mild dairy products, chocolate, tobacco, some alcoholic, beverages, fruits, vegetable, textiles, clothing and footwear. These are the sectors in which the developing countries have a competitive and comparative advantage. High trade barriers imposed by the industrial countries on agriculture and processed food imports along with agricultural subsidies have contributed to the decline in developing countries' share of World Trade in these commodities". (*Hindu Survey of Agriculture*, 2002). Needless to say, that the ideal of an open, equality and transparent rule-based multilateral trading system is still eluding the developing countries because the developed countries with their dominance thwart the efforts of developing countries from getting greater market access in world trade for their products, using all types of non-tariff and technical barriers, anti-dumping rules and rigid environment and opaque high product standards for preventing exports of the developing countries. For instance, UNCTAD estimated as many as 22 non-tariff barriers operative in Japan, as many as 16 in the EU, 1 in Australia, 4 in U.S.A. and so on. Analysis of the past eleven years since the establishment of WTO in 1995 brings out that the new trading system seems to favour the developed countries and leaves the developing countries to fend for themselves in the emerging competitive globalised market-based world economic environment. The developed countries have evolved many new instruments of safeguarding their interests while the developing countries have been forced to implement their commitments of liberalisation. Aditya Sen has rightly observed, "The purpose seems clear: developing countries have a market potential and that must be tapped to the advantage of rich countries. The history of clash of interest indicates that the real economic purpose is never revealed, it has to be understood as it unfolds itself" (Sen, Aditya, 1998). The developing countries have realised the fact that their hope of getting additional market access in agriculture, textiles and clothing and movement of natural persons under services, which had been committed by the developed countries can not be fulfilled because the developed counties have tended either to under implement these commitments or to implement in a manner that makes the fruits of liberalisation available to them. These countries felt need to safeguard their interest themselves and so there are many such issues on which there are different between the developed countries and the developing countries from the very beginning of the WTO's inception. The clash of interest has initiated cold war between the developed countries and the developing countries.

India's Expectations from the Uruguay Round

In pursuit of solving the acute economic problems accumulated until 1991, the integration of Indian economy with the world economy was felt highly desirable and so Indian policy makers took steps in this direction through adopting the policy of LPG and accepting the WTO's membership. India has honoured its commitment for trade liberalisation with the hope of getting benefits declared in the Preamble to the WTO Agreement which is most attractive and promising. The preamble to the WTO Agreement opens by declaring that the purpose of relations between WTO members entails. "Raising standards of living, ensuring full employment and a large and steady growing volume of real income and effective demand, and expanding the production of and the trade in goods and services, while allowing for the optimal use of the world's resources in accordance with the objective of sustainable development, seeking both to protect the environment and to enhance the means for doing so in a manner consistent with their respective needs and concerns at different levels of economic development" (Kumar, Jeevan, 2005). For Indian policymakers this preamble appeared to be pregnant and they failed to conceive any predicament. On the contrary, they considered the new free trading order as a panacea of all economic ills like low economic growth, low standard of living, poverty, unemployment and what not. In their opinion Dunkel Agreement is likely to result in significant expansion in world trade as a result of removal of trade barriers and reduction of tariffs. India's exports will increase by at least 2 billion annually over and above the normal growth in exports. Their logic behind such thinking lies in the fact that the WTO brought textiles and agriculture into the mainstream of GATT and so it was expected that market access would increase in these two areas resulting in an increase in global trade in general and Indian trade in particular. India continued predominantly to be an agrarian economy even after more than five decades of Independence and so agro-products along with textiles has remained dominating items in its trade volume. And the developed countries like the U.S.A., EU and Japan have been the major export destinations of Indian exports. With the inception of the WTO India expected a lot in terms of market access for these two products. The Indian policymakers were so optimistic and hopeful that they forgot the two necessary ingredients for raising our exports—product development and market research along with other important preconditions like improvement of infrastructure, more particularly port-facilities, surface transport and communications. Their high estimation, lies in their profession regarding the favourable impact of the WTO on fast modernisation of agriculture and industries in order to meet the challenge of competitiveness in the international market. And once Indian farmers and traders attain standards similar to those in the developed countries, they will stride forward in a big way making its presence effective in most markets of the world. Besides these, in their vision the service agreement opens a new scope in our favour because it places the cross border movement of 'natural persons for supply of services on the same footing as other modes of supply of services. Thus, India estimated a lot in terms of free trading order leading to better resource allocations and the economic system getting long run benefits in the form of adjustment of the system to technological innovation, new production structures and changing pattern of competition.

India and Ministerial Conference

For directing and providing guideline there is a provision for having a high decision-making body within the WTO which meets at least once in every two years. Till date,

Ministerial Conferences have been held in Singapore (Dec. 96), Geneva (May. 98), Seattle (Nov.-Dec. 99), Doha (Nov. 2001) and Cancun (Sept. 2003) respectively and the sixth one which is going to be held in Hong Kong (China) in the last month of this year is due.

The Preamble of the Marrakesh Declaration (1994) stressed on special consideration on the exports interests of LDCs in the application of import relief and other measures permitted by the GATT and also to provide them with increased technical assistance in development. A large number of WTO Agreements recognize the need for ensuring preferential market access for LDCs and developing countries. The ministerial Conference held in Doha in November, 2001 witnessed the fact that the WTO members agreed to place development issues at the forefront of the new round of trade liberalisation negotiations. The Doha Development Agenda which stressed on market access, agricultural reforms, reduction and elimination of trade barriers on consumer and industrial goods and liberalisation of trade in services marked the first time that developing countries' interest were placed at the centre of multilateral trade negotiations. But negotiations have been deadlocked over issues of fundamental importance to developing countries—market access in agriculture and labour intensive products, intellectual property in medicines and the nature of special differential treatment for developing countries. Naturally, the US-EU trade distorting policies for agriculture as well as market access for non-agriculture issues have come as a 'jolt and a challenge for India and other developing countries. According to a study by the' International Food Policy Research Institute', US farm policies deprive developing nations of $11 billion annually in last export income. In case of the EU, the figure is $20 billion (Thakur, R.N. 2003). Thus, the developed countries tried their best to use the WTO as such a weapon by which they can hold over the markets of the developing countries any how in the name of liberalised trading order or globalisation. India and other developing countries are worried for the breach of commitments by the developed countries in the field of agriculture, industry and services. And such type of cold war remained no longer hidden. The cold war between the developed countries and the developing countries converted into an open war under the leadership of India, China and Brazil at the time of the Ministerial Conference held in Cancun in September, 2003. India and other developing countries realised the fact that if commitments done in Doha and earlier ones to establish a fair and market oriented trading system that is free of distortion in agriculture and other sectors, the gains to India and other developing countries would be substantial. And perhaps nearly 200 to 500 billion dollar as additional income to the developing countries as result of trade liberalisation calculated by the World Bank came true. The World Bank states that a deal that addresses the concerns of developing nations could spur growth and reduce poverty by as much as 144 million people by 2015. But all the anticipated gains have completely eluded the developing countries including India. Setting aside all development issues that formed part of Doha Agenda led to a united opposition from the developing countries. India along with Brazil spearheaded the developing countries battle at the WTO's fifth Ministerial Conference, attacking the draft document that was-seen by them as 'one-sided' in favour of the European Union and the United States and ignoring their interests. Our then Commerce Minister Arun Jaitley asked, "How can we expect developing countries to reduce tariffs on a number of items to between zero and 5% as provided in the draft when the distortions against which such tariffs were supposed to compensate are sought to be enhanced". (In *Hindustan Times*, Sept. 15, 2003). About 98 least developed countries—Africa, Caribbean and Pacific and Cancun nations forced the EU-US dominated WTO ministerial summit to end demanding exclusion of Singapore issues—investment, competition policy, trade facilitation and transparency in government procurement in the work programmes. EU-US negotiators' strategy to bank on the differences among the developing countries, lack of bargaining power or money power, to further their interests failed. The biased attitude became clear in the discussions on the 'three pillars' of domestic support, export competition and market access.

India's Stand

Our Commerce Minister Kamal Nath has expressed his stand in both Houses of parliament strongly in these words, "We are determined to pursue our interest vigorously. We are determined to ensure that as negotiations proceed based on the framework agreement our core concerns are adequately addressed" (*The Times of India,* Aug. 17, 2004). The framework agreement adopted by the WTO Executive General Council on August 1, 2004 in which Kamal Nath said that we had been able to achieve all our major objectives in this framework agreement which was the first major step to break the impasse in WTO talks after the collapse of the Cancun Ministerial Conference. It laid down principles and criteria for moving forward in the ongoing Doha round of trade negotiations. On the most important contentious issue of trade distorting domestic support in agriculture it is heartening to take down that the developing countries have succeeded in extracting an immediate commitment in the form of 20% reduction in the developed countries' overall trade distorting support in the very first year itself. How the framework agreement would benefit India in the crucial area of agriculture, it is said that it provided for elimination of all forms of export subsidies by an end date. At the same time the flexibility available to the developing countries like India to provide certain subsidies for export of agricultural products would continue to be available for an even longer period beyond the elimination of export subsidies by the developed countries. The World trading order under the WTO has been beneficial for India and that it had to fulfil certain obligations on the understanding that other countries too would commit themselves to the same, said our Commerce and.Industry Minister. When India decided to accept and adopt the World trading order, its exports stood at less than $32 billion. A decade later, they had doubled to $64 billion and now the country looking towards doubling exports in five years. "This year we are already set to cross $75 billion. All this translates into more employment opportunities and greater economic activity with its concurrent benefits," said Kamal Nath (*The Hindu*, Dec. 28, 2004). Really, this is a very rosy picture, particularly when we make a comparison between the pre-WTO and post-WTO period. Just before Dunkel Agreement the World's total exports are about 3800 billion US Dollar of which India's exports are only 19 billion - 0.5% as against China's 85 billion, America 450 billion, Germany 430 billion and Japan 350 billion. In spite of all these it is seriously felt that there is need for taking a fresh look at the anti-dumping and anti-subsidy initiatives taken against India to give a boost to trade to the desirable extent.

Recent Developments

For the success of the Sixth WTO Ministerial Conference in Hong Kong, a mini-ministerial meeting was held in Dalian in order to reach realistic agreements on key issues, including agriculture. The spirit of Dalian meeting has found best expression in the words of Zhang Xiangchen, the spokesman for the meeting. Our expectation is that Dalian informal Ministerial meeting will be successful one which will promote the Doha Round. Really, the two Asian giants—India and China, accounting for 40% of the world population have forged a common front to fight attempts by the EU and the US to deprive the two fast growing economies of the special benefits of their being developing countries under the WTO regime. Both the countries are working together in the WTO to thwart attempts by some advanced industrial countries to divide developing countries even as they seek to step up bilateral trade. Hopes have just been revived for 600 million Indians engaged in farming and millions of others in poor countries. A comprehensive proposal tabled by G-20 countries led by India in Geneva on the 8th July, 2005 found broad acceptance in Dalian meeting by 30 WTO players as the basis for working out a world farm trade deal under the ongoing round of multilateral talks with developed countries which had-mouthed platitudes for Africa and Asia. Glaneagles, found it hard to dismiss of hand the G-20 proposals for cutting their huge farm subsidies and providing market access to farm produce from the developing countries, faced with a forceful articulation by ministers from the developing world, especially our Commerce Minister, Kamal Nath, the leaders of the developed countries had to grudgingly announce their general acceptance.

Trade diplomats were enthusiastic that Tuesday's deliberations (12th July) marked a breakthrough on the central issue of agriculture which holds key to the success of the entire trade opening round. A year had passed after WTO members reached a framework agreement in July last on how to conduct the complex negotiations spanning agriculture, industrial products, services and WTO rules but very little progress was achieved since then. It was agriculture that was mostly blocking the talks from making headway. Of course, India has successfully geared up for pre-WTO meeting in China.

Opportunities

No doubt, the objectives of WTO are to provide an opportunity of having a multilateral umbrella which is transparent and fair, based on the agreements negotiated and agreed upon by all signatory member countries, which give certain facilities to the developing countries over a period of time to be integrated with the global system. These objectives are yet to be reached. "India has much to gain if WTO plays its game fairly, if signatories to it are sincere, there is no chicanery, deceit, foul play and dumping. There is gain and they must gain who have comparative advantage endowed by nature and their efforts" (Mishra, J., 1997). India is an agricultural dominated country having comparative advantage endowed by nature and so Indian agriculture is in a position to make major gains in the export market. Actually, the WTO with its liberalisation policy in the world trade in agriculture has provided huge opportunities for Indian agriculture in which India has an inherent strength to dominant in global market. National Council of Applied and Economic Research has identified 17 agricultural products in which India has comparative advantage over other agricultural producing countries. With increasing awareness, more agricultural products are entering this list, such as floricultural and horticultural products. Exports in this sector are estimated to grow at 20-25% a year. India is the third largest food producer in the world. In the production of wheat and fruits as well as vegetables its position is second in the world. About 9% of the total world fruits and vegetables is produced in India next to China. It has the potential to emerge as a major exporter of seed. India is a vast country having large differences in soil and climatic conditions which make it possible for the country to grow a variety of crops to meet the external demand in the global market. In many of the countries diverse agro-climatic conditions and cheap labour rarely exist and so growing vegetables and fruits and some other agricultural products is a costly affair for them whereas India has a comparative advantages in growing these commodities. Spices also play a vital role in export of agricultural commodities. The export earning of spices was Rs. 1702 crores in 1999-2000 (*Economic Survey,* 2000-01). It is worth noting that in India agriculture accounts for nearly a third of its gross domestic products, but agricultural products constitute just about 1/8 of its total exports. The share of agriculture and allied products in total exports has come down from 20.5% in 1995-96 to 12.3% in 2002-03. Naturally, this declining trend compels us to think over the reality. Next in line of expectations is textile producer and readymade garments which have been ruled by the quota regime MFA. The Uruguay Round of trade negotiations tried to bring textile trade into the mainstream by removing the quota on textile' items in three stages resulting in an increase in trade in textiles. Its share has hovered around one fourth of India's total exports. Moreover, since India's total farm subsidies are below 6% the provision of reducing subsidies will have no effect in India. According to the *Economist* of London, developed countries of the world were heavily subsidising their agriculture, much against the spirit of the WTO In 1998, the average subsidy per farmer in U.S. was $30655. On per hectare basis, it was $550 (Rs. 23650 at the old rate). The total amount of subsidy paid in 1998 to U.S. farmers was $97.3 billions (equal to Rs. 418400 crores) which was much more than the total value of all farm products in India, Japanese farmers with 72% subsidy. South Korean farmers with 60% subsidy and European and US farmers with subsidy between 25% and 60% will be worst sufferers. This will ultimately increase the price of agricultural products in developed countries benefiting India's products in respect of prices in the international market (C. Renuka; Nagesh Kumar, 2001). The challenges posed by economic liberalisation policy can be converted into an opportunity by developing alternative extension approaches or by broadening the existing approaches. Few years back, it was reported that livestock products such as ghee and milk had been imported and sold at comparatively lower prices than the Indian livestock products but this sector can be saved from these problems by changing our extension approach as early as possible. It is heartening to take down that in terms of total milk production, our country ranks first, in total meat production it ranks seventh and in broiler production it ranks sixth in the World. Further, our egg production stands second in Asia and fourth in the world. Still, we are far behind in terms of per unit productivity and so due to the low productivity, the cost of production is high as compared to the international market. For converting the challenges posed by the WTO into an opportunity, a paradigm shift is required from production orientation to quality and cost orientation for enhancing the contribution of livestock to national economy and external trade. Hereby it is worth noting that in the ED, for instance, products like meat, milk and cream, cheese and rice continue to carry tariffs of over 120% resulting in making the potential gains to a country like India elusive. And so India must insist on the maximum tariffs, not to be more than 50% on any tariff line relating to agriculture. For availing the opportunity created in the post-WTO we need to wake up and change our approach soon in the direction of making our industrial products more competitive. If we do not do so, the Indian market will be flooded with surplus product from the developed countries, which will ruin the economy of India. Already the process has started in certain areas such as toys, electric tubelights and other electronic items. Needless to say that we have the feasible potential to be competitive in gainsome way in agriculture, industry and service sectors. And we need to take a positive stance at negotiations based on the principles of liberal economics and try to take advantage of multilateral trade and investment opportunities. Hopefully, India alongwith certain other leading developing countries has taken certain steps to make pressure on the developed countries to be honest partners in international trade and leave their foul game through adopting many new instruments of safeguarding their national interest. Hopefully, now after the Cancun Ministerial Conference held in September, 2003, the developed countries have become aware of the reality that the developing countries interest can no longer be ignored openly and completely. The reality lies in this fact that since Doha and Cancun, the voice of the developing countries has become a force to reckon with. Undoubtedly, the voice of the developing countries is being heard today and if it is so, India will take advantage of new opportunity created by the WTO.

Challenges

While the broad objectives of WTO in bringing about a rule based liberalised world trading system are laudable, the practical experience of the emerging policy actions is in sharp contrast to the perceived expectations. The theory of competitive advantage based on labour-endowments and factor intensities, is no longer valid. Competitive strengths are determined by the new factors such as access to information knowledge intensity and aggressive policies in marketing. The need is to focus attention on challenges we face in integrating our economy into the evolving global economy. It appears that international relations are power relations and countries which are politically and economically very strong, exercise the maximum influence in shaping the international economic order. Poorer countries are at a great disadvantage in influencing the course of events and very often, they end up adjusting to a framework agreed to among the major economic power. (Singh, P.N. 2003). While some significant opportunities are emerging under the WTO regime, it is very good sign that India is not unaware of "the challenge (that) arise out of the fact that the WTO bears the birthmarks of a deeply divided world, in which the developed countries have many unfair advantages over the developing countries. India is (therefore) playing an active role in mobilizing other developing countries for removing these disadvantages and establishing a truly just, equitable and fair world trading order." (PM, 2001) It is but natural that combination of exogenous and endogenous factors which are prevalent in the developing countries including India, has generated apprehensions and fears among them on their ability to withstand the challenges of this highly complex multilateral trading environment even under the rule-based WTO. The exogenous factors consist of the ravages of volatility in exports and exchange rates, oil price hike mounting external debt, effects of economic downwing of their major trade partners due to ongoing global recession and other adverse developments in the multilateral trade environment whereas weak domestic resource base, technological backwardness, unskilled labour, undeveloped economic and financial infrastructure, political, ethnic and social turmoil etc. are such endogenous factors which work as fuel to the fire for constraining their export competitiveness. Indian economy is now guided more by market forces as well as competition and less protection. In such economy the price mechanism allocates resources to different industries on the basis of their conceived profitability, but these companies or industries do not supply what the market needs, they could literally out of existence. That is why, Joseph Schumpeter spoke of competition as "the gale of creative destruction"—creative, in so far as new products, new processes and new technologies come into existence, and destruction because those not so equipped to face competition now face extinction. (Mehta, Fredle, 1995). In fact the WTO engineered globalisation is a double edged weapon. It provides, on the one hand, with opportunities to share the international market and on the other hand, exposes the economy to competition from foreign supplier in the domestic market and force its production to adopt more efficient techniques of production.

Globalisation of Indian agriculture was institutionalised in 1995 through various agreements such as Agreement on Agriculture (AOA), Agreement on Sanitary and Phytosanitary Measures (SPM), Agreement on Technical Barriers to Trade (TBT) and Agreement on Trade Related Intellectual Property Rights (TRIP) signed under the auspices of the WTO. The agriculture sector since 1995 is passing through number of challenges. Agriculture, with 26.8% contribution to the GDP at current prices, 18.5% to the total exports and providing employment to nearly 66% of the work force, continues to be the most crucial sector of the Indian economy. But in the post-WTO era, survive or perish is now becoming the buzz word of the developing countries like India. Of course it is very dismal picture for Indian economy because its growth is key to achieve sustainable higher rate of growth in the country. One incremental percentage growth in agriculture leads to an incremental income generation of Rs. 10.000 crores in the hands of the farmers (Mukhopadhyay, Jiban K. 2004) Such vital sector is facing challenge. The main fear is that with the implementation of WTO agreement and trading provisions, Indian market will be flooded with different farm goods from foreign countries at a rate much lower than that indigenous farm products leading to a death-blow to Indian farmers. Our expectation regarding reduction or complete withdrawal of domestic and export subsidies by the developed countries resulting in raising prices and bringing immense increase in agricultural exports of the developing countries including India appears now to be a day dream. Due to lower productivity, low yielding seeds and primitive tools of production and market support, the Indian farmers cannot stand in competition with the farmers of the developed countries, and above all only 6% subsidy to agriculture in the country below the 10% permissible limit as per WTO provision on the one hand and on the other hand the removal of Quantitative Restrictions (QRs) on imports give birth to apprehensions about inundation of domestic markets by imports. Moreover, the average operational holding is around one hectare, only with two-thirds of lands solely dependent on monsoon rains for cultivation Indian farmers with all the constraints have to compete with farmers from the rest of the world with operational holdings exceeding 1000 hectares generally. Besides, due to the low productivity, the cost of production is high as compared to the international market, The yields of major crops in India when compared to some other developed countries, leaves a lot to be desired. India compares poorly with other developed countries like Indonesia and Vietnam, leaving out China which outsmarts India by a large margin for all crops. Likewise, we are still far behind in terms of per animal productivity. Our cows produce only 987 kg. of milk per lactation as compared to 6273 kg. in Denmark, 5289 kg. in France, 5462 kg. in U.K.

5938 kg. in Canada, 7038 kg. in U.S.A. and 11000 kg. in Israel (Hegde, N.G., 2001). Our beef and pork yields are half the world average. Further, the goat and sheep meat yields are also less by 20-25%. (Birthal, R.S. 2000) What makes the situation worse is the fact that Japan has recently rejected Indian mango due to various organic and inorganic residues on mango skin for which Indian exports have to import special machines for further processing. Similarly, rice sent to Iran was rejected on the basis of sub-standard quality. The EU banned import of fish from India due to lack of adequate hygiene protection especially in canning of crustaceans. The instances of a large number of cases of suicide by farmers in Andhra Pradesh and Karnataka are clearly indicative of the seriousness of the situation at least in some parts of the country. Thus, the agricultural sector in India did not produce the expected outcome, thereby not actualising the desired results because the obligations that were accepted by the developed countries especially in the agricultural sector did not get materialised. Moreover, the recent study reveals that India has lost comparative cost advantage in consumer oriented agricultural products (fish and fish preparations, vegetables and fruits and manufactured tobacco), medicinal and pharmaceutical and in essential oils and perfume materials toilets, polishing and clearing preparations as indicated by slow increase in our country's exports as compared to world export in these commodities. In this concern a recent report on India by Michael Porter can be quoted. "Competing based on resource endowments is increasingly vulnerable to shifts in exchange rates, competition from other low wage and resource nations, and technological progress that minimizes basic factor inputs. Competitiveness depends on the productivity with which a nation's resources are deployed, (which implies) quality features as well as cost, total cost, not just labour cost." To meet the challenges posed by the WTO it is now an urgent need for the Indian agricultural research system to respond to the demands of the international agriculture market because in terms of quality, most of the Indian farm products do not conform to international standards on account of sanitary and phytosanitary restrictions, processing and packaging specifications and so on. The food sector in the country will also have to face new challenges in the new patent regime. Different processes and products will become patentable. There is, therefore, a need to document all the traditional processes as well as products with a view to reduce the number of controversies over claims for patent rights. (Katti, Vijaya, May 2005)

One of the most daunting challenges facing India to provide employment not only for the additions to labour force but also to reduce the backlog accumulated from the past cannot be expected to be solved in the present scenario created by the WTO under the LPG model. It was hoped that once the economy is freed from the regime of controls, quotas and licenses it shall result in a much higher growth rate of GDP and a significant expansion of employment. Economic liberalisation was hailed as a panacea in the same manner as socialism was considered to be the only method of achieving growth with social justice during the first four decades of development. (Datt, Ruddar, 2004) Dr. Man Mohan Singh as a Finance Minister has expressed his optimistic outlook in this regard in these words: "We are creating a macro economic environment in which industry speeds ahead with growth rates of 12% or more, generate more jobs and higher levels of wages and incomes through increased productivity." Even when the success is measured only in terms of an increase in the rate of growth of national income only (GDP/GNP), an analysis of the experiences of the developing countries clearly shows that there has been success for only a few, mixed for a few others like India, and failure for a large number of countries (in Latin America, Subsahara Africa, Transitional economies of eastern Europe and some East Asian countries after the 1997 crisis) but what has happened to unemployment, poverty and inequality, The "Wealth of a Nation", wrote Adam Smith more than two hundred years ago, is determined by "First, the skill, dexterity and judgement with which the labour is generally applied, and secondly, by the proportion between the number of those who are employed in useful labour, and those who are not employed." Unfortunately, the proportion of these who are not employed is increasing in the post-WTO era or say the post reform era. Actually, the restructuring programmes aimed at moving the economy towards a more sustained growth path create an adverse impact on employment. Unemployment due to restructuring is expected to arise from three sources; closure of some of the economically non-viable enterprise, downsizing of the workforce in other weak units and adjustments in labour force in perfectly healthy enterprises necessitated by changes in market conditions and/or technological innovations. In fact, the structural changes initiated in India are expected to lead higher rate of growth and efficiency but at the same time in this process many enterprises find themselves unable to stand competition or to adopt to the technological changes, rendering large number of workers redundant, underemployed and unemployed. Of course, the trade liberalisation, one of the reform strategies launched with the aims of making the Indian economy more competitive and efficient has almost proved failure in giving answers to many ills faces by the economy. According to UNIDO, "many developing countries are today adopting an approach to industrial development, based on an export-oriented trade strategy, with the hope of creating the dynamics for overall economic growth and improving income levels. Unfortunately, their enterprise, more often than not, lack the skills and knowledge required to compete in international markets. Moreover, government policies, institutions and infrastructure are frequently inadequate to private necessary support for related trade and production activities." In such scenario we fail to achieve our targeted economic growth and the LPG model bringing about capital intensive technology provides jobs only to a few skilled persons. The unskilled labourers of both organised as well as unorganised sectors are bound to suffer from widespread unemployment. Undoubtedly, computer revolution has provided jobs opportunities for the Indians in western countries but at the same time it has minimised jobs in our country. Like some other developing countries India did not encourage indigenous technology and permitted selective imports especially for priority sectors. As a result the imported capital intensive technologies creating distortion in our economy are making our challenge to solve unemployment problem more grave. Due to several reasons such as severe competition from MNCs, inadequate accessibility to institutional credit, poor capital base, inadequate standardisation of products, component parts and sub-assembles, inaccessibility to technology, information and management practices etc. a substantial increase in sickness of SSI units especially after 1995 is found. The small scale sector which produces a wide range of more than 7500 products and contributes 40% to exports of manufacturing products and providing employment to 199.65 lakh persons in over 35.72 lakh units has started withering with the opening of the economy when looked at the data if presents a disturbing picture. According to an estimate foreign imports have killed off as many as more than 40,000 small and medium industries. The enormity of the problem can be more plainly gauged by looking at the absolute number of jobless i.e. as many as 7 million during 1990-98 (nearly 4 million in the rural and about 3 million in the urban areas) Estimates based on the data available from NSSO indicated that there occurred a significant deceleration in the growth of employment in the post-WTO regime. Using the Current Daily Status (CDS) criterion, employment grew at 2,89% per annum during 1983-84/1987-88 and 2.50% during 1987-88/1993-94 but only at 1.07% during 1993-94/1999 2000. Corresponding growth rates of GDP for these periods were 4.2, 5.8 and 6.7 per cent. It appears that a higher growth rate could not result in faster growth of employment, on the contrary a faster growth led to a lower employment growth, particularly during the period 1993-94/1999-2000. (Papola, T.S. 2004) Recent estimates from the Planning Commission, however, suggest that the process of deceleration of employment growth has been reversed during 2000-2002 when employment growth has been over 2% per annum, with an average of 8.4 million jobs added per year, as revealed by the preliminary results of the 8th Round Survey of NSSO. Encouraged by these results, the Planning Commission is now hopeful of achieving the Tenth Plan target of 10 million jobs per year with the realization of the envisaged GDP growth rate of 8%. We have to recognize that our current domestic saving rate of 22% of GDP is not sufficient to achieve the growth target of 8% for the 10th Five Year Plan which requires an investment rate of 28-30% of GDP. How can we ensure the growth of job opportunities on such a large scale in the present scenario? Moreover, the moot point is that job losses are occurring in areas where the incidence of wage employment is of high order, where market driven propensities operated much more ruthlessly and where in the days to come the domestic economy has to bear the burden of increasing competition from abroad. So far as trade liberalisation enforces closures rather than efficiency at a micro-level, or switches domestic demand away from home produced goods to foreign goods at a macro-level, it has an adverse effect on output and hence employment which is magnified through the multiplier effect. There is contraction of employment in some sectors without a compensatory expansion of employment in other sectors. And as employment elasticities of output decline employment creation slows down. For any given level of employment, the globalisation of prices without a globalisation of incomes also threatens livelihood. Moreover, in India rapid population growth and unfavourable ratio of the working age group to the dependable population affect the economic health of the country adversely and make employment scenario tiff to be solved. (Jha, B.K. 2004) The most pitiable condition found in the present globalised era is of growing unemployed persons. It is a well known fact that unemployment weakens the bargaining position of the workers and enables employers to employ workers on terms and conditions of work that they dictate. This widens the scope for growing inequality of income in the society as a whole. There is enough scope for the rich to be richer and the poor to be poorer. The Director General of the International Labour Office sketches the following disturbing picture. "In 1960, the income gap between the wealthiest fifth of the world's population and the poorest fifth was 30 to 1. By 1999 it was 74 to 1" (ILO, 2003). Among broad layers of the world population, there is growing sense that a central feature of today's globalised world economy is "the egregious and historically unprecedented degree of global inequality in income and wealth, and life chances broadly construed. Although inequality between the North and the South is particularly extreme, there are stark (and rapidly deepening) inequalities within each of these regions as well" (De Martino, 2000). Stiglitz has rightly observed that the west acting through international institutions like the IMF, the World Bank and the WTO has seriously mismanaged the process of globalisation and by following its advice many developing countries are actually worse-off now than they were before. There is now indisputable that the benefits of globalisation and liberalisation have been less than its advocates claim. During the post-WTO era the problem of unemployment, poverty and inequality has emerged as a great and grave challenge for our country. Really, poverty and unemployment are twin brothers and it is also important to remember that the greater the inequality, the less the poverty reducing effect of growth. And so growth is pro-poor when it is labour absorbing and accompanied by policies as well as programmes that mitigate inequalities and facilitate income and employment generation for the poor particularly. Former member of Planning Commission Prof. G.S. Bhalla has also focused light on the undesirability of a jobless growth. In fact, we are now experiencing the devastating effects on our economy in the form of growing inequality between countries and within country, falling incomes and employment of those with less skills and failure of social security of the growing marginalised and vulnerable group and the last but not the least the danger to livelihood.

Undoubtedly, global and liberalised market and trade offer opportunities for all but opportunities do not guarantee the desired results. In our case, even granting the fact that our trade to GDP ratio has increased to the post reforms era from about 1.3% of GDP in the early nineties to about 20% of GDP in 2001. However we have a long way to catch up with the levels achieved by the developed countries and the Asian Tiger. Undoubtedly, there are some areas e.g., cotton, textiles, garments, leather goods, gems and jewellery, light engineering products etc. where we are seen to be a visible player but the markets of all such products together occupy a small proportion of the total global exports. In a vast majority of other product categories accounting for 85-90% of global exports, and which are essentially of high value and/or technology intensive manufactured goods, India's presence is evidently negligible. Although it is heartening to take down that India seems to be emerging as a major exporter of IT products and services surging at 40 to 50% exports growth of this sector, with the projection of $50 by 2008 from the present about $6.5 bn, even in IT sector it is the software segment where India is doing extremely well while the hardware sector remains in its nascent stage. In a nutshell Indian industry is also facing challenge of globalisation and liberalisation and it has lost its status as the 10th largest industrial power in the world.

Concluding Remarks

First of all we need to get rid of myths and misconceptions surrounding the origin and evolution of the international trading order in the form of WTO. It is but misconception that today's developed countries have grown fast economically because they follow the policy of free trade. It is a matter to remember that there is no free trade in real sense. The WTO is not based on the practice of free trade but it is regulating international trade on the basis of negotiated rules which do not reflect free trade for all products and all countries. Although the major developed countries, to further their own interest, have always advanced free trade theories, they maintain protection significantly in major sectors like agriculture and textiles in which the developing countries have a comparative advantage. The developed countries protected their domestic industries behind tariff wall and adopted tariff liberalisation only when the domestic industries have become sufficiently strong or efficient to stand up to competition from imports. So Indian policymakers need not be befooled with the idea that they can get rid of their problems with the help of the international institution's prescription. They should not forget the stark reality that there are some hidden loopholes in the Uruguay Round of Agreements which provide the scope for non-implementation of the agreements in their proper spirit. There is no denying the fact that the WTO is subject to the overriding influence of the USA and the European countries and all the agreements seem to be discriminately more or less to protect the interest of the developed countries. Undoubtedly, if UR package is completely implemented, world trade would increase 12% recording as large as 60% in cloth product, 20% in agriculture, forestry, fishery and 19% in processed food and beverages. It was also estimated that the real income would increase between $212 billion and $274 billion i.e. around 1% of World GDP. All things are right only when UR Agreements will be translated into practice properly and honestly having no bias for the developed countries which seems to be difficult if not impossible in the present scenario. A dedicated honest effort by all WTO members is highly desirable for invigorating the trade liberalisation process that fosters the formation of a more open, peaceful and prosperous world. Perhaps time has not matured for leaving the developing countries to fend themselves in the emerging competitive globalised market based on world economic environment. There is need to accept the valuable suggestion of Anne Krueger the IMF's first Deputy Managing Director, who said, "... but that more needs to be done for those who have left behind." She emphasized that "globalisation will continue to be vehicle for closing the gap between the industrial countries and the rest of the world". There is a need for deeper appreciation for large but developing countries like India. It calls for a series of positive steps in terms of granting GSP, reducing non-tariff barriers and also contingent remedies. Our concerning ministers have asked major players of international trade to take a fresh look at the anti-dumping and anti-subsidy initiatives taken by India to give a boost to trade but their response cannot be considered satisfactory. The hollowness of nation-state, the growing inequalities, the rising unemployment, insecure informal economy, growing working poor, declining earning of the unskilled, destruction of environment and deprivation of basic human rights in the post globalised and liberalised era are enough for one to rethink for an alternative paradigm Instead of the ongoing development paradigm of the LPG strategy in which market is temple and money is God. There is no reason as to why we are hesitating to think over the New-Gandhian approach to development for permanent solution of our problems. Our past experiences of a decade reveal the fact that it is wrong to presume that global welfare is maximised by economic growth, and the latter is best achieved through economic and political liberalisation. On the contrary there is adverse repercussion on our economy particularly rural economy. Till date our blind faith in the intention of the developed countries stands in the way of facing challenges created during the post-WTO era. To be globally competitive, a country must be blessed with two favourable factors i.e. an unlimited reservoir of talented and skilled labour as well as an abundance of capital available for new projects. India has never been charged with an inadequate supply of the most scarce resource of all-talent. Sir William Pyrie, the Executive Vice President of the IFC has said in this context that India has some of "the most creative entrepreneurs the most dynamic business leaders and the sharpest financial brains in the world". (Palkhivala, 1998) But at the same time it is not less true that about 44% of all workers in 1999-2000 were illiterate and 22.7% had schooling only upto the primary hike (Sharma, Alakh N. 2004). Today India is competing with only half its manpower, with the rest of the world. Since half of the Indian population is literally illiterate. For globally competitive we are in dire need of value based education. We should always remember that our country will be built not with brick but with brains, not with cement but with enlightenment, when Indians are better educated will know how to behave better as workers and to discharge with greater responsibility their duties as citizens. India has a great future if it joins hands with all other developing countries to protect their interest and livelihood; gives proper and bold answer to the developed countries and works together for arresting the trend to set aside the concerns of developing countries as nontrade issues. If they are in need for ensuring technology transfer from the developed countries to the developing countries and so they have to make pressure on the developed countries for this through a separate technology agreement. What is highly desirable is to lessen the dominance of the developed countries in a policy decision and agreements on different issues. Undoubtedly, all these steps if taken boldly to safeguard our interest we can face the challenges created by the WTO to a certain extent but for permanent solution new Gandhian approach to development can no longer be ignored. For job oriented economic growth, for economy having the level of social welfare of Sweden, Civil Liberty of Holland, income distribution of Norway, the health care of Germany, the public culture of France and security of employment of Japan, restricting our industries to make them more productive and globally competitive is neither only remedy nor enough. Above all it is well to note that active membership of an international organisation and total sovereignty for a member is incompatible. A degree of surrender of national sovereignty is basic to any cohesive international cooperative arrangement. And so there is no reason for any kind of hesitation in pondering over the statement of our former Prime Minister Charan Singh who has boldly suggested to adopt the Gandhian approach to development in these words "If we have the good of the people as a whole at heart, by and large, in a capital poor and labour-rich country like India, there is no escape from an economy Mahatma Gandhi advocated. His kind of economy will not in the present context but will also serve all our other aims, that is, it will provide maximum employment, ensure equitable distribution of national product and promote a democratic way of life." (Singh, Charan, 1981) Of course, we cannot remain indifferent to technological progress oh international level and international situation and so only alternative left in my vision is to adopt the neo-Gandhian approach to development conceptualised by the former President of India called PURA.

REFERENCES

Mishra, Jagannath (1997) *My Vision for India's Rural Development*, Vikas Publishing House, New Delhi, p. 02.

Papola, T.S. (2004) Globalisation, Employment and Social Protection, *The Indian Journal of Labour Economics*, Vol. No. 3 p. 5.

Datt, Rudra (2004) Employment and unemployment In India, *Bihar Economic Journal*, Cent. Vol., p. 13.

Jha, Birendra Kumar (2004) Growth and Employment Trends in the Economy, *Bihar Economic Journal*, Conf. Vol., p. 54.

C. Renuka & M. Nagesh Kumar (2201) SWOT Analysis of Indian Agriculture, IEA Conf. Vol., p. 104.

Prime Minister (2001) Quoted from the PM's speech at the conference of Chief Minister on WTO and Agriculture and Food Management held in New Delhi.

Palkhiwala, Nani A. (1995) Booklet Forum of Free Enterprise.

Mukhopadhyay, Jiban K. (2004) What India Needs, a Booklet Forum of Free Enterprise.

Thakur, R.N. (2002) WTO & Issue of Agriculture, *Bihar Economic Journal* Conf. Vol., p. 44.

Sharma, Alakh N. (2004) Globalisation, Labour Markets and Poverty, D.T. Lakdawala Memorial Lecture.

Singh, R.N. (2003) A Decade of Economic Reforms in India and Challenges Ahead, Prof. R. K. Sinha Memorial Lecture.

Kumar, Jeevan (2005) Free Trade vs Fair Trade, *Southern Economist*, Vol. 43. No. 20.

Singh, Charan (1981) *Economic Nightmare of India*, p. 441.

Sen, R., Development Alternatives for India in the next Decade. Dr. Kedar Nath Prasad Memorial Lecture.

Hindustan Times, Sept. 15, 2003.

Times of India, Aug. 17, 2004. *The Hindu*, Dec. 28, 2004.

Hindu Survey of Agriculture, 2002.

5

SMALL SCALE INDUSTRIES IN THE GLOBAL GAME OF WTO IN THE GLOBAL ERA

*Birendra Kumar Jha**

Prologue

Globalization in Indian context is to be judged on the parameters like job-creating rather than job-less, poverty reducing rather than ruthless, inequality decreasing rather than inequality enhancing, environment friendly rather than futureless, participatory rather than voiceless and culturally entrenched rather rootless, to make it desirable as well as feasible. It is to be judged on the basis of its positive impact on job creating, poverty reducing, equality enhancing and environment friendly sector like small industries. It is needless to say that India is a developing country facing chronic problems like unemployment and underemployment, poverty and inequality from the very beginning but these problems have attracted the attention of policy makers, planners, academicians and others recently when they found no solution to those problems even in the post-global era. Of course, globalization has been deemed as the panacea for solving all those problems but on the contrary it has aggravated them in comparison to pre-reform regime. In such scenario one is forced to think that there is something wrong in giving due

* Reader & Head, Department of Economics, DBKN College, Narhan, Samastipur, Bihar.

priority to the most desired sector like small scale industries in the course of economic development of the country during the pre-global as well as post global era similarly. The history of India is development experience indicates that both Nehruvian socialistic vision and LPG (liberalization, privatization and globalization) vision prove in effective in the Indian case and so them is need to evolve a new model that goes beyond the Russian and American models. A model in which market is not considered to be temple and money is God as found in American model or say LPG strategy, is highly desirable globalization in Indian context—Globalization in India has commenced ever since the commencement of the economic reforms in 1991 which were crisis driven and it has commencement of the economic reforms in 1991 which were crisis driven and it has become mandatory since the country signed the WTO agreement in 1995. In order to pulling the economy out of the crisis of unprecedented balance of payment and mounting fiscal deficit India initiated economic reforms. Liberalization, privatization and globalization (LPG) are the three fillers on which the edifice of the new economic policy has been created in India (Jha, B.K. 2005). At the beginning of the 21st Century globalization—a term first used by Theodore Levitt in 1985, has become a household name in all corners of the world.

Although globalization means different things to different people, it can be defined as a process of increasing openness, growing economic interdependence and deepening economic integration between countries in the world economy. The mainstream case for openness rests on the belief that free trade enhances welfare because it results in a more efficient international division of labour as nations are forced to specialize in the production of goods and services in which they have a comparative advantage. Undoubtedly, the main beneficiaries of free trade are consumers who do not only pay lower prices for goods but also have choice. If an assumption of increasing returns to scale is made, the gains from trade can be shown to be still greater (Upadhya, V. 2004). Trade openness is an important measure of globalization, which connotes pervasiveness, inclusiveness and sweepingness with epidemic and pandemic implications in international trade and financial relations. In its global scope and sophisticated operation, it is referred to as the new face of liberal capitalism. It is a new avatar of the 18th Century imperialist colonisation, and exploitation and the 20th century neoliberal economic fundamentalism (Gandhi, Jagdish, 2005). Globalization is a new word for which Marxists call imperialism and we people in the third world refer to it as colonialism.

Operation of globalization brought into its wake both opportunities and challenges opportunities for growth and challenges for overcoming the weakness on all fronts of national economy. Developing countries that have seized the opportunities offered by globalization have fared better than ever in history. China and India, which account for more than half the population of the developing word have raised more than 350 million people above the poverty line in the last decade. But countries that have failed to climb on the globalization band wagon, mainly in Africa, have suffered the most. Moreover, globalization must not be interpreted to mean the more absence of trade or investment barriers but it implies empowering the people of a country to participate in the global economy. It implies that countries have developed the policies, institutions, infrastructure and educational levels that enable its people to latch into the opportunities created by globalization. It is but true that globalization has raised both apprehensions and expectations, more often the former than the latter. It has had differential impact on labour markets and employment across countries and regions. In general, the experiences of a very large number of countries both developed and developing show that growth of employment has declined and informalisation of the labour market has increased leading to greater insecurity in employment conditions and declining social security mechanisms. Inequality in income/earning within and across a large number of countries has been yet an other consequence of globalization (Sharma, A.N. 2004).

It is really worrisome that the implication of the globalization process for developed countries and developing countries are not similar. The Human Development Report, 2002 observe "Globalization is forging greater interdependence yet the world seems more fragmented between rich and poor, between powerful and powerless between those who welcome the neoglobal economy and between those who demand a different course. Economically, politically and technologically the world has never seemed more free and unjust." The gulf separating Indian and other developed countries is so wide that it will take for India much more time in a standstill world to catch up with them.

Table 1. World Disparity

Country	*HDI Rank*	*GDP (Bns)*	*PCIs*
U.S.A.	6	9837	34142
Japan	9	4842	26755
U.K.	13	14.5	23509
China	96	1080	3976
India	124	457	2358

Source: HDR, 2002.

Not surprising, recently the RBI Governor said "Despite all the talk, we are nowhere even close to being globalized in terms of any commonly used indicator of globalization infact we are still one of the least globalized among major countries however we look at it". But by expanding the boundary of the market beyond the boundaries of the nation state through economic globalization, the concentration of market power moves beyond the reach of Government. To date globalization has only perpetuated poverty, widening inequalities, ecological degradation, sustained militarism and deepened crisis of democracy. For the people of the third world including India, the dream of securing a full time job has not been realized. Thus, LPG vision cannot solve our problems and we are forced to follow the very opposite path of globalization although it has shown a shining face on economic growth front which has crossed the Hindu Rate of Growth, jobless economic growth is neither desirable nor feasible.

Small Scale Industries and Its Growth

What to talk of India, throughout South Asia there is clamour for industrialization South Asia is intellectuals like their counterparts in the West, believe the present high level of development in advanced countries is the result of changes set in motion by the Industrial Revolution. Even Burma, Thailand and Malaya, where there is more land and better opportunities for raising the levels of living, the long-range outlook demands that substantial industrial expansion must take place to improve conditions for a rapidly increasing population (Myrdal, Gunnar, 1972). In India from the beginning two major schools of thought on the approach to industrialization stand out clearly while the Nehru Mahalanobis model favoured a strategy of building basic and key industries with the expectation of maximizing growth rates over the long run. Gandhiji did not think that large factories would be able to solve either the problem of unemployment and underemployment or that of providing the Indian masses with their basic requisites. As is well known, ultimately the Nehru-Mahalanobis strategy prevailed over the Gandhian approach and the first five year plan embarked upon an ambitious programme of building a net work of basic and key industries whose gestation period was long whose investment requirements were too heavy, and whose growth propelling effects were to follow after long time gaps. Nevertheless, the merit of Gandhian philosophy was not completely lost to the Nehru-Mahalanobis school of thought (Chadha & Sahu, 2005). It is needless to say that the relative merits of less capital intensity and more labour absorption capacity among others have endeared SSI sector to the policy makers as an instrument to achieve a variety of economic objectives such as employment generation, production of mass consumption goods, balanced regional development, equitable distribution of income etc. Moreover, for reasons of social and political expediency, if not entirely economic efficiency, India has chosen to walk on two legs and this core element of industrialization strategy has stayed on till today. The multidimensional merits of SSI for an underdeveloped economy like India were identified by the policy makers right from the beginning and the sector got official recognition as soon as Indian attained independence through its Industrial Policy Resolutions (IPRs) of 1948 and 1956. The IPR of 1956 outlined, "The Government of India would stress the role of cottage and village and small-scale industries in the development of the national economy. In relation to some of the problems that need urgent solutions, they offer some distinct advantages. They provide immediate large scale employment, they offer a method of ensuring a more equitable distribution of the national income and they facilitate an effective mobilization of resources of capital and skill which might otherwise remain unutilized. Some of the problems that unplanned urbanization tends to create will be avoided by the establishment of small centres of industrial production all over the country. In the policy an emphasis was given on encouraging small industry to acquire sufficient vitality to be self-supporting and its development to be integrated with that of large scale industry. In the policy the need for improving competitive strength of small industry through technology improvement and modernization was also fall and stressed.

Even in the global era an exclusive policy for small industry was introduced in August 1991 in which there was no any major deviation from the past found but the policy intended to promote competitiveness of the sector more than anything else and unlike the past, instead of containing mere intentions of Government the policy has proposed clear guidelines to deal with the three major areas of concern for the sector: *(i)* finance *(ii)* marketing and *(iii)* technology. There is no denying the fast that SSI was assigned a crucial role in India is economic development strategy by all the Industrial Policy Resolutions in the pre- as well as post-economic reforms period.

All industrial units whose investment in plant and machinery does not exceed Rs. 1 crore (in original cost) are notified by the Government of India as small industry and are grouped as belonging to small scale industry. The capital investment which was less than Rs. 5 lakh in 1950 has been raised to Rs. 1 crore, but the limit for investment in tiny units has been fixed at Rs. 25 lakhs. However, recently, the investment limit has been increased to Rs. 5 crore in the case of 41 hi-tech and export oriented products of hosiery and hand loom sub-sector, to make them globally competitive. Moreover, industry related services have also bee include in the list provided that investment in such enterprises does not exceed Rs. 0.5 million. The Indian small industry sector can be divided into two classes: traditional small industries and modern small industries. The former industries include village industries, handloom, handicrafts etc. Whereas the latter include small consumer products to sophisticated machine tools and electronic goods. Coverage of the third census of small scale industries, unlike the earlier two is much wider as it encompasses both registered and unregistered units.

SSIs have emerged as an engine of growth in several developed and developing economics of the world. Of course, SSIs are a key component in economic life, not only because of their number and variety but because of their involvement in every aspect of the economy, their contribution to regional development, the complementary role they play in support of the large sector and on the ground of innovativeness and adaptability. Even in those industrialized countries of Europe and America where the large scale industries dominated the scene during sixties and seventies, there has been major turn around and SSIs are now in the centre stage. How surprisingly it is, but true that "At a time when the West of Europe, the birth place of the modern industrial system, was inhabited by uncivilized tribes, India was famous for the wealth of her rulers and for the high artistic skill of her craftsmen". Prof. Weber wrote: "The skill of the Indians in the production of delicate woven fabrics, in the mixing of colours, the working of metals and precious stones, the preparation of essences and in all manners of technical arts, has from very times, enjoyed a worldwide celebrity". These observations signify the prominence and the glory of the products of the cottage and small scale industries. But the advent of modern large scale mechanized industry, the imposition of restrictions on Indian trade by the British rulers and deteriorating socio-economic conditions led to the decline of SSIs. Soon after the attainment of independence this sector has staged a grand recovery and in now well entrenched on the path of progress towards great expansion.

According to the third all Indian census of SSIs (2001-02) there were 105 lakhs industries units working in small scales sector employing 249.3 lakhs personnel at the end of March, 2002. The total output (gross) of small scale sector is placed at Rs. 282269 crore in 2001-02 (at current prices), which was roughly 13 per cent of total GDP. Traditionally, a large proportion of SSI units in India are under the unregistered sector for example, out of a total of 105 lakh units in SSI in 2001-02 more than 91 lakh (87%) belong to the unregistered sector. However, so far as the total gross output of the SSI sector is concerned, the registered sector accounts for the major share 72 per cent. The share of SSI output (gross) as percent to total GDP in 2001-02 stood roughly at 14 per cent. As per the latest census information, the SSI sector generated employment of as many as 249 lakh people, of which around 33 lakh (13%) employees are women. In terms of the total workforce based on 2001 population census, SSI employment constitutes a share of 6.2 per cent (GOI, 2003). The size (based on gross output) distribution of SSI is highly skewed; more than 70 per cent of the units employing roughly 39 per cent of the SSI workforce produced an output below Rs. 1 lakh. In contrast, less than 4 per cent of the units produced a gross output of over Rs. 50 lakh. Besides, the top 20 industries account for more than half of the total units of SSI. During 2001-02 the export of SSIs stood at US $ 14.199 million, the registered sector generated around 87 per cent of total exports. Despite changes in the definition and coverage of SSI units during 1987-88 to 2001-02 i.e. the period between the 2nd and 3rd censuses of SSI, the registered sector recorded an annual average growth (compound) of 12 per cent production at current prices. During the same period, employment in the registered sector increased by a compound growth rate of 3.8 per cent (Rao, K.S.; Ramachandra, Das; Abhiman & Singh, A. Kumar, 2006).

For seeing how policy changes introduced during the period of economic reforms and initiatives towards globalization have affected the growth of the SSI sector let us look at the performance of this sector over the decade since 1990. According to the SIDO production in this sector grew at a relatively low rate during 1991-1994, growth rate was higher than 10 per cent from 1994-95 to 1996-97, around 8 per cent in the subsequent four years and declined to around 6 per cent during 2001-02. Overall, the growth rate has been lower in the 1990s than in the earlier decade during which it averaged to over 10 per cent per annum. Employment growth averaged to 4,8 per cent during 1991-92 to 2001-02 as compared to 7.6 per cent per annum between 1980-81 and 1990-91 (DCSSI, 2002). Thus, it appears that the growth of the SSI sector experienced a set back in its growth during the period of economic reforms, but, at the same time, the sector seems to have shown a greater resilience than the large sector in overcoming the challenges of globalization. For instance, the growth of industrial sector as a whole declined during the 1990s, averaging at around 6 per cent while production in the SSI segment grow at a higher average rate of about 8 per cent per annum (ISID 2004). One reason could be that a large part of the SSI sector has no links with the sectors directly affected by reforms in industrial regulation and trade regimes and the other reason may be in the continuation of protection in terms of reservation and fiscal and financial incentives even during the reform period (Papola, T.S. 2004). It is well recognized and documented that an overwhelming majority of the units consists of micro-enterprises and are in what is broadly christened as informal or unorganized sector. About 99.5 per cent of units are in the category of tiny enterprises having fixed investment in plant and machinery of less than Rs. 25 lakhs each and 96 per cent have below Rs. 10 lakhs of such investment (DCSSI, 2004). Average fixed investment in plant and machinery of the SSI units works out to be Rs. 1.47 lakhs. Over 90 per cent employ 7 workers or less each. Average number of workers employed by a SSI unit is 2.37.

Table 2. Performance of SSIs during 1994-95 to 2004-05

Year	*Number of units in lakh*			*Production at current price*	*Employment in lakh*	*Exports at current price in lakh*
	Registe-red	*Unregis-tered*	*Total*			
1994-95	11.61	67.99	79.60	122210.00	191.40	29068.00
1995-96	11.57	71.27	82.84	148290.00	197.93	36270.00
1996-97	11.99	74.22	86.21	168413.00	205.86	39248.00
1997-98	12.04	77.67	89.71	189178.00	213.16	44442.00

1998-99	12.00	81.36	93.36	212901.00	220.15	48979.00
1999-00	12.32	84.83	97.15	234255.00	229.10	54200.00
2000-01	13.10	88.00	101.10	161289.00	239.09	69797.00
2001-02	13.75	91.46	105.21	282270.00	249.09	71244.00
2002-03	14.68	95.42	110.10	311993.00	261.38	86013.00
2003-04	15.54	99.68	115.22	357733.00	273.14	NA
2004-05	16.38	15.00	31.38	399020.00	245.75	NA
Average annual growth rate 1994-95 to 2004-05	41.08	50.24	48.90	226.50	28.39	195.90

Source: Ministry of Small Scale Industries, Govt. of India.

Despite policy bias in favour of SSI and comprehensive institutional network, Indian small industry achieved little in terms of technological progress, although during the pre-reform period the performance of this sector was successively hailed as its contribution in terms of employment, production and exports increased remarkably. It is needless to say that performance of the SSI sector has, to a large extent been attributed to the comprehensive policy followed by the Government for the promotion of the sector. As is well known, this policy consisted of several elements including exemption from excise duty, special provision and concessional rates of interest on bank credit, infrastructure support including provision of space in industrial states, capital subsidy for technological upgradation, preferential and exclusive purchase of products by government and above all, reservation for exclusive manufacture for a large range products. There have been periodic changes in the elements of policy. Of late, there is an emphasis on improving the competitiveness and market development and towards a gradual reduction in purely protective measures such as reservation (Papola, T.S. 2004). Since 1991, SSIs have been undergoing a transition from 'protected growth regime' to 'competitive growth regime'. Hence, the institutional support and policy measures have been aimed at increasing growth of SSIs though strengthening and enhancing of their competitiveness. This is evident, for instance, in the comprehensive policy package for SSIs and Tiny sector, announced on August 30, 2000 by Government. Other things being the same, a higher productivity implies a higher competitiveness by way of capturing a larger market share, both domestically and globally. A higher competitiveness induces a higher growth through larger employment and investment and lack of competitiveness results in closure and sickness through loss of productive employment and investment. It is at this juncture that the Government initiated several measures to strengthen the competitiveness of small industry, in pursuance of the small industry policy, 1991. Most of these measures are related to technology upgradation and modernization, finance and marketing. It is perceived that the future role of this sector will be based on competition, productivity and efficiency. In regard to SSIs, the 10th Plan which has set the following national level performance targets for increasing total production from Rs. 624363 crore to Rs. 1401939 crore, total employment from 20.1 million persons to 23.7 million persons and total exports from RS. 73600 crore to 126000 crore, also recognizes the emerging external constraints in terms of WTO and market access among others but it is expected that the small sector will grow faster in a more competitive environment due to their cost advantage and will be profitably access the larger markets in the liberalized trade regime.

SSIs in the Global Game of WTO

Gone are the days when small scale industries in India have been functioning admits protected environment i.e. reservation for products manufactured by these units, quantitative restrictions of imports, wall of high import tariffs, preference in sanction of loans, concessions from the government and purchase of products by government departments. Gone are the days when SSIs sector had to face competition only on national level and those industries had to compete only with the large units within the country. Even in competing with the large units these industries were not required to face rough weather due to the liberal and biased attitude of the government in their favour for flourishing. But now all the previous scenario has changed to a great extent.

The decade of 1990s was an eventful one in terms of policy changes nationally as well as internationally. These new developments have changed the economic environment for SSIs considerably. This sector is facing a tough challenges for its survival and growth in this period of globalization in which survival of the fittest has become the buzz-word in the Indian industrial sector today. The Development Commissioner of SSIs (DCSSI) in the year 2001-02 conducted a census of small scale enterprises in the country and found 822893 total number of sick units in SSI sector in India in which 192326 were found registered and 630567 unregistered units. The number of sick small scale industrial units in December 1980 was 23,149 which increased to 145776 in December 1986 showing 6.3 fold increase in six year period (Singh, Shrawan Kumar, 1990). Thus, this showed an increasing trend in the number of sick small scale industries. What to talk of SSIs, after introducing liberalization policies and globalization Indian industries are being closed one by one and there is a decay of SSIs on a large scale. Actually, SSI sector is now exposed to global environment of competition. Consequently, small scale industries fate is at stake. Aligarh, once known as lock-town of India has been shut down. Firozabad, known for glassware products is producing only bangles these days Maharashtra artisans are jobless. Lamps manufacturers in Gujarat are searching for cheap raw materials for their production. Shivakashi's cracker production has been severally affected. Plastics, electronics, sanitary or be it textiles, future of every industry is insecure. Indian power loom and handloom industries are also under crisis. About 50 per cent such industries are closed now and the remaining are running under lower capacity production. Our edible oil is also in crisis due to import of oil from foreign countries, India's toy industry too is losing its ground to Chinese products. Electronic toys, soft toys, decoration toys, plastic toys and other items have virtually elbowed out the Indian toys from the markets. Cheap artificial flowers and fruits are also very commonly demanded in the Indian market. Be it a village, town or metropolitan city, China made low priced cheap quality goods have invaded all regions of Indian markets. Over Rs. one million worth of Chinese goods are sold in India everyday. This is only an estimate market insiders claim that the estimate is highly conservative. Instead, they assert, if could will be over eight to ten million rupees a day. What may be figure, there is no doubt about the fact that China invades India's small scale industries because in India the production process is distributed in different sectors, which increases the cost. This is not the case in China as all the goods are produced under one shed. The labour laws in China are in favour of manufactures and in India everything is opposite. Surprisingly, China made items have flooded the Indian market, giving rise to an alarming situation for SSIs but the government is busy day-dreaming about our growing economy whereas local manufacturers are worried about their daily income. This can be imagined when one comes to know that lord Ganesha also made in China comes in different shapes and sizes, far more attractive than the traditional ones compelling Maharashtra's is traditional artisans who have been making the Ganpati idols for almost a century now, gradually being elbowed out of the trade. Fate of the West Bengal artisans who have been making the idols of Goddess Durga for centuries for the Puja festival is no different. The survival and success of SSIs depends mainly on their being competitive and cost effective besides maintaining desired quality. The sector faces formidable challenges today not only from multinationals but also from large domestic players. The gradual and impending application of WTO regulations has added to its woes. WTO agreements do not discriminate on the basis of size of industries. After implementation of WTO norms, reservations may have to be withdrawn, preferential purchase and other support measures may not be available. As a result SSIs have to compete not only with the large units within the country, but also with cheap imported products. India being the founder member of WTO, has been following the decisions scrupulously and has opened the floodgates for foreign goods to enter in the Indian market but developed countries are using various protectionist measures like anti-dumping duties, unilateral change in the rule of origin and unjustifiable foisting of environment issues. It is but true that as import from India affects the interests of developed countries particularly the United States, a number of environmental and human rights issues were raised in order to imposing a bar on the import of Indian produced particularly in the small scale sector on the plea that in their manufacturer child labour is involved. Thus, WTO provisions relating to tariff and non-tariff barriers, non-permissible subsidies, intellectual property rights, safeguard measures have affected the small scale sector less favourably and more adversely and at the same time these provisions have enabled the developed countries to push their exports to India at a much faster rate. And as a results the SSIs sector which accounts for over 33 per cent of export is in jeopardy. The rule of survival of the fittest is being applied to this sector which is suffering from lack of infrastructure facilities, technological obsolescence, imperfect knowledge of market conditions and above all inadequate availability finance and credit and in their game only a few able ones will be able to survive. Chinese goods started entering into Indian market six years ago but within a short span of time, it put a big challenge before the Indian manufacturers and their future survival. In the year 2004, India is total trade with China crossed $13.6 billion with imports for approximately $5726.67 millions. Not only that, the entry of multinationals in ordinary consumer goods like ice cream, agarbati manufacture, food processing, mineral water etc. is also adversely affecting the SSI sector since these were the traditional areas of this sector. Is it not true that the entry of powerful coca cola and pepsi in soft drinks have struck out practically all small units engaged in the manufacture of aerated water? MNCs which prefer low technology, quick profit yielding and large volume products with regular demand throughout the year, continue to swallow SSIs and strike them out from the market. In such scenario the peculiar characteristics, inherent strengths, latent capabilities and survival instincts of survived industries in this sector have enabled them to weather surroundings problems so far. And the need of the hour is to strengthen the competitiveness of SSIs so that this important sector can face the challenges of globalization and avail opportunities created in the global era.

The process of liberalization and market reforms has created opportunities for the development of small scale industries, too although certain small industries have been hit hard due to WTO related developments. There are certain sectors like information technology which have improved their performance as a result of trade liberalization because it is opened up new business opportunities for them. With removal of QRs, imports of raw materials, machinery and technology has become easy for the industrial sector in India. As such, SSIs may now have strategic alliance with entrepreneurs in any country, buy required technology from any source, explore alternate sources of raw materials,. This will result in reduction in the cost of production and ultimately will make such industries more competitive with MNCs. The increased competitive pressure on large scale industries to specialize and focus on core activities and leave the rest to be done by small scope industries. Even foreign large scale companies are outsourcing good quality products from small and medium enterprises at very cheap cost. Indian small industries may grab this opportunity by becoming vendors or sub-contractor to these MNCs.

With liberalization of the economy and its assimilation into the globalized world economic order, the number SSI units has been steadily growing. For instance, units in SSI sector have gone up from 2.57 million (31.03.1995) to 11.86 million (31.03.2005) with an average growth of 5 per cent each year. Production of SSI units at constant prices (1994-95) has been recording an impressive average growth of 125.22 per cent during the period from 1994-95 to 2004-05. SSI units were generating 13.94 million employment avenues as on 31.03.1995 which increased to 28.29 million as on 31.03.2005 with an impressive average annual growth of 28.39 per cent. Exports of SSI sector also jumped from US $ 8,07 billion in 1993-94 to US $ 13.13 billions in 2002-03 (B. Appa Rao, V. Krishna Mohan and K.B.D. Sobha Rani, 2005).

Conclusion

Undoubtedly, the SSI sector has proved its mettle even in the changed liberalized economic scenario of the country but the emerging economic scenario in the changed liberalized and competitive economic environment has necessitated structural and fundamental changes in the policy framework put into place for the development of this vital sector of the economy. Accordingly, there has been a shift in focus from protection to promotion and for converting the challenges into opportunities for reaching new heights, the need of the hour undoubtedly is to provide sustenance through suitable measures to strengthen SSI Sector. Despite the fact that SSIs responded and proved mettle even in the WTO environment they face a variety of problems due to the unorganized nature of this sector, lack of data and information, use of low technology sometimes obsolete technology and poor infrastructure in the country. The NSS report of the latest round (56th round) which pertains in the year 2001 throws considerable light on the problems faced by entrepreneurs in this sector. Shortage of capital in the capital scarce nature of our economy emerges as the most serious problem along with other problems like marketing, non-availability of raw materials, power cuts, lack of infrastructure, competition from the larger units etc. Although competition from imports is not specifically mentioned, this problem has been lately emerging in quite a serious form in the Indian scenario. In order to face the problem of competition from imports under the WTO regime, it would be necessary to permit reservation policy for small scale industries to continue for some time while simultaneously taking all steps to ensure that during the interim period, productive efficiency of SSIs rises sufficiently to cope with import competition. The profile of SSIs in terms of size, product composition, location, productivity and growth suggests consolidation of the restructuring process where in better performance is achieved through shifting from vary small units to relatively larger within SSIs, from unregistered to registered industries, and from non-cluster to cluster identities. The contribution of SSIs to the overall health of the economy is being questioned on the grounds of their low productivity and factors like technology, access to resources and inputs, general macro-economic atmosphere etc. emerge as important determinants of-productivity. As much as 40 per cent of value added and 50 per cent of employment in the SMEs are reported to be concentrated in the low productivity (labour productivity less than Rs. 3000 per worker per annum in 1980-81 prices) segments and activities (Shah, 2002) and about 25 per cent of the workers in the unorganized manufacturing sector are said to be seriously underemployed (Oberai and Chadha, 2001) under such conditions the sustainability of SSIs is argued to depend on improving labour productivity through technological upgradation. Undoubtedly, any technological upgradation which is a costly proposition due to capital scarcity in a developing economy like India will raise productivity and improve performance but efficiency upgradation appears more viable, effective and lucrative compared to technological upgradation and efficiency upgradation depends more on training, experience and familiarity of the workers rather than the range of tools that complement them (Rajarshi Majumdar, 2004). It is argued that future of most SSIs lies in linkage with large enterprises resulting in ensuring marketing of their products as well as inducing productivity increases through technological and product upgradation but unfortunately enough, in the UP survey only 9.43 per cent of sample enterprises were found to have such linkages. Switzerland can be cited as an example where many separate village families make wheels or other parts of watches which are assembled in the big factories and go to make the famous Swiss Watches. Japan can also be cited as another example where sub-contracting is widespread particularly in producing special kinds of paper, lanterns, fountain pens, cutlery and light engineering products.

It is true, if there are no improvements or innovations, we will keep our economy backward and will not reap as much advantage out of our physical resources as we can. But again we will do well not to forget—in the development of countries which are today highly industrialized, technical innovations were adopted only when they were economically justified. Labour was replaced by capital wherever this was justified by a reduction in cost. Introduction of automatic machinery in our country, where unemployment prevails in its ugly form, would certainly mean not a reduction, but a considerable increase in costs (Singh, Charan, 1965) "I would favour" said Mahatma Gandhi, the use of the most elaborate machinery, if thereby India's pauperism and resulting idleness could be avoided (Gandhi, 1921).

In the global game of WTO "India has much to gain if WTO plays its game fairly, if signatories to it are sincere, there is no Chicanery, deceit, foul play and dumping" (Jagannath Mishra, 1991) but it would be a day dream in the prevailing scenario when the provisions of WTO protect the interest of developed countries and globalization is charged for widening the gap between rich and poor, increasing inequality, unemployment as well as poverty. There is need to force WTO to rectify the biased provisions to ensure equal opportunity for all and to support the developing countries like India.

REFERENCES

1. Mishra, Jagannath (1997). *My Vision for India is Rural Development*, Vikas Publishing House, New Delhi.
2. Singh, Charan (1965). *India's Poverty and its Solution*, Asia Publishing House, New Delhi.
3. Jha, B.K. (2005). WTO & India: Opportunities and Challenges, 88th IEA Annual Conf. Vol.
4. V. Upadhyay (2004). Globalization and Developing Nations, *Political Economy of WTO Regime*.
5. Rao, Mohan and Sobharani (2005). Implications of WTO on SMEs, 88th Annual Conference.
6. Ghosh, R. and Mitra, A.S., Problems and prospects of SSIs, *Journal Economic and Social Development*, Vol. IN-I.
7. Chadha and Sahu (2005). 'Rural Industrialisation in India', *Plural Transformation in India*, IHD, New Delhi.
8. Papola, T.S. (2004). Small and Micro Enterprises in a Gloablized Economy, Conf. Isuse, Vol. 47, No. 4.
9. Balasubrahmanya (2000). *The Indian Economic Journal*, Vol. 47, No. 2.
10. Rao, K.S.R., Das, A. and Singh, A.K. (2005). Commercial Bank Lending to SSI, *EPW*, Vol. XLI, No. 11.
11. Majumdar, R. (2004). Productivity Growth in Small Enterprises Conf. Issue, Vol. 47, No. 4
12. Gandhi, Jagdish (2005). Globalisation Emerging Imperative, *Globalisation and Contemporary Eco-scenario*.
13. Gunnar, Myrdal (1972) *Asian Drama: An Inquiry into the Poverty of Nations*, Vintage Book, New York.

6

INDIAN HIGHER EDUCATION AND WTO AGREEMENTS: PROBLEMS AND PROSPECTS

Dr. V.S. Kulkarni[1] *and Prof. Medha Tapiawala*[2]

I. Introduction

In today's knowledge driven society, the acquisition of "human capital" has become increasingly significant and relevant as every one at every place is moving from physical assets to knowledge assets. Now competition in any area is a competition in knowledge. According to the recent study conducted by the World Bank in 192 countries, 'Physical capital and natural wealth' account for only 16% and 20% respectively of the total wealth, while 'human capital' accounts for the rest of the wealth.

The Indian economy with a series of economic reforms since 1990's has become open and technology driven. The economic reforms have slightly elevated India's position in the world's human development Index (HDI) position from 138 in 1994 to 127 in 2003 (UNDP 2005).

Globalisation has lead to the death of distance and as such the world has not only shrunk but also become highly

---

1. Reader and Head of the Dept. of Economics ,KMC College, Khopoli, Raigad, India, 410203, email: drvsk58@rediffmail.com
2. Sr. grade Lecturer, Dept. of Economics, Guru Nanak College of Arts Science and Commerce, Sion, G.T.B. Nagar. Mumbai 400037, email: medha020@yahoo.com

competitive. The signing of GATS agreement by Indian economy has called for tremendous amount of challenges and opportunities in the service sector that is basically knowledge based. One of the major areas of GATS agreement is in such highly knowledge based higher education, which has made higher education saleable service internationally. In this context the paper attempts to analyse the problems and prospects of Indian higher education under GATS agreements.

II. Nature of Agreement in Education Sector

There are five areas covered under the agreement—

1. Primary education
2. Secondary education
3. Higher education (including post secondary, technical and vocational education services)
4. Adult education
5. Other education (testing and certification)

The modes of supplying educational services under the agreement includes—

1. Cross border supply (e.g. distance education)
2. Consumption abroad of services by consumer traveling to supplier's country (e.g. student studying abroad)
3. Commercial presence (e.g. a campus abroad)
4. Presence of natural persons from supplying country in consuming country (e.g. faculty teaching abroad).

The GATS agreement has thus led to the open competition between Indian and foreign providers of higher education. The moot question for Indians is whether we can face global competition? The answer is 'no' in the context of present scenario of higher education suffering from major weaknesses and problems listed below.

Low Equity and Access

Despite impressive quantitative growth in enrollment, it is disheartening to note that only 22% of families today are the first generation learners in higher education and only 6

% of the Indian population in the age group of 18-23 is in higher education as compared to 51% in OECD countries and 21% in middle-income group countries

Poor Quality

By and large higher education is neither relevant nor effective to face the challenges of globalization, as most of the courses in general higher education stream, are outdated, dubious, and have no relevance to the needs of the society or individual.

Policy and Infrastructural Problems

The problems include:

1. Uncontrolled and unplanned expansion of general higher education stream mainly due to highly subsidized and open door admission policy.
2. Poor infrastructural facilities.
3. Rigid and inflexible general education courses framed with traditional mindset and neglecting global technical advancement even in updating technical education like western world.
4. Lack of co-ordination between Universities and Government and poor Industry-institute partnership and Omni-presence of the Government in administrative and academic life of Universities as it is a major funding agency
5. Lack of integral urge to accept change and dynamic mechanism, on the part of Universities, as a competitive knowledge industry.
6. Lack of Teachers' accountability, research and innovation and shortage of funds for research.
7. Poor inter-sectoral allocation of funds by the Government on higher education as compared to primary and secondary
8. Degree biased and Exam oriented approach.

The above problems lead to the challenges like creation of mass educated unemployment; deterioration of quality, influx of foreign institutions with sound infrastructure and better quality of increased competition and last but not least increasing social disparities among youth.

III. GATS Challenges

With the GATS agreement in one area of higher education, we observe following major changes and challenges in the Indian economy.

1. Environment for Higher Education and Earners

Since the GATS meeting at Uruguay 1995 the ADC's have started the task of selling higher education in LDC's very systematically through advertisement, seminars, testing services, delegations engaging agents in LDC's to market their education. They also provide visa assistance, pre-departure orientation programme, part time job opportunities, tie-up programme, franchises, exhibition and fairs, scholarships, hostel facilities, special counseling centers, information through internet etc. But we had hardly made any efforts to attract foreign students, except very few technical and management institutions. As a result there has been a continuous rise in Indian students going abroad.

2. Role of Foreign Providers of Education

Education accounts for about $2.5 trillion of the world's economy each year. The higher education service market was estimated about $40 Bn. in 2005, with U.S. holding largest market share.

Table 1: Distribution of Foreign Students of the World

Countries	*No. of Foreign Students*
USA	4,50,000
UK	2,10,000
Germany	1,80,000
France	1,30,000
Australia	1,20,000
Japan	51,000
India	5200*

Source: *figures of 1996.

3. *Investment and Funding in Research and Development*

The relative advantage of a country in the global market comes out of its investment in R & D, technology and higher education. The investment through state in higher education and R & D in the western countries including US, compared with India is sufficiently high. Following table indicate the poor picture of Indian expenditure higher on education.

Table 2: Students Entering Higher Education in Different Countries

Countries	*Net Entry Rates*
Finland	71%
New Zealand	70%
Poland	62%
Australia	59%
Netherlands	51%
UK	46%
Korea	45%
US	43%
Japan	39%
France	37%
Germany	30%
India	7%

IV. Strategies for Reforms

As on today, maximum numbers of foreign students, studying in US are from Asian countries (54%). India alone accounts more than 80000 students representing about 14% of total foreign students studying in US. A Large percentage of middle income groups are unlocking their investment in real estate, gold, savings etc. and deploying the same in quality foreign education. On the contrary there is a continuous fall in foreign student entering India. For e.g. in 1995-96 there were 6535 foreign student and the number came to 5200 in 1996-97 and to only 2800 in 2001-02. This clearly shows that we are not well prepared in trading our higher education abroad. The basic reason includes poor quality, outdated courses, poor propaganda of our specialized courses etc. among others.

Following is the Strategies for Reforms:

1. Mind set for complete revamping of non- professional higher education by restructuring the curriculum to meet the global market.
2. Fine tuning of existing technical education to face the global competition more confidently.
3. Recovering the real cost of higher education from the beneficiaries, for quality improvement and cost consciousness. However the weaker sections should continue to get long-term low interest loans than subsidies.
4. Autonomy in higher education must be encouraged for better quality, higher competitiveness and self-financing.
5. More funds for research by the Govt. are desirable. However Institute-Industry linkages and Tie-up funding is necessary.
6. Efforts should be made to tap global market to export our educational talents. (Indian technocrats at Silicon Valley in the U.S. is a classical example).
7. Development of 'India Branding' & making global exposure of best institutions of higher educations for foreigners (Best IIT's, Software Co's, & Management institutions can do this at present.)
8. Accessing global talents for best quality higher education through collaborations, & inter university–institution exchange programme, based on the principle "Collaborate & co–exist than compete".
9. Continuous up-gradation of quality of teachers & institutions through accreditation is required to improve the quality. Finding out new channels of resources mobilizations through alumna, corpus funds, Tax-exemption for education fund contributions, attracting foreign students etc. and best utilization of available resources.

10. Stress on specialized areas like yoga, Philosophy, dance, music, traditional medicinal educational like Ayurveda etc.
11. Strong will power & hard work: The real strength of India lies in her people. They can accept any challenges & achieve success too. Late Mr. Dhirubhai Ambani (Reliance) & Mr. Narayan Murthy (Infosys) are prime examples to show that how common most man can rise to the top of the heap.
12. What is needed is a change in the system itself. More importance should be to given application- and project-oriented methods. Creativity must be encouraged among children. Teaching and evaluation should change accordingly.
13. Making open learning system more popular & vocationalised, as it is simple, flexible, effective, economical & accessible to all regardless of 'who' & 'where' they are.
14. Rise in Fees:- The share of the Govt. in financing higher education has increased from 49 % in 50-51 to 90% in 96-97. The higher education system even today is highly subsidized. It is interesting to note that the quantum of subsidies is enjoyed more by upper income groups, both, in general and professional higher education. There need to be equity and also cost consciousness of the fees paid.
15. Autonomy:- The colleges and Universities should try to develop built-in-flexibility in financial matters. Autonomy is the best solution that provides both academic and financial freedom.
16. The social responsibilities must not be forgotten. It includes access, equity and national interest. Here the Government, corporate bodies, charitable institutions and NGO's should play key role.
17. Indian authorities must request for assistance from UNESCO and other world bodies for improving educational infrastructure in the country. This has been done in other WTO agreement on sanitary and

phytosanitary measures and Technical agreement barriers to trade.

18. For a smooth transition to the new liberalized environment, encourage WTO member countries to have more students–exchange programme so that exchange student could become the young ambassador, messenger and promoters of our educational services in their respective countries.
19. Infrastructure up gradation of our premier and import competing institutions must be done on a priority basis so that they can effectively compete with foreign institution based in India. India must propose gradual liberalisation.
20. Existing reputed educational testing services will have to be modernized. To compete with testing service such as say GRE, GMAT, and TOFEL, our reputed testing services such as CAT, GATE, JEE NET and others must be upgraded and modernized.
21. A note on National Knowledge commission rport-2006:

The NKC's first annual report outlines some concrete steps to the problems of Indian higher education. They include–

a. Creation of about 1500 universities by2015 against present existing 350 universities, including creation of upto 50 National Universities that can provide education of highest standards.
b. Establishment of an independent regulatory authority for higher education (IRAHE)
c. Raising the government's support to higher education from the present 0.7% of GDP to between 1.5% and 2% of GDP by 2012.
d. Encouraging public–private partnership
e. Academic audit, assessment and accountability on regular basis etc.

V. Conclusion

The review clearly indicates that the present scenario is not much conducive for marketing our higher education internationally. There is no question of going back to protective model because the present world situation will benefit only to those who compete and excel. We have to be the part of globalization and benefit from the opportunities offered by the global system.

This call for a big push and TQM strategy in applying necessary reforms in academic, financial and administrative aspects of higher education sector, so as to make it globally feasible and competitive. Systematic and collective efforts by government and private sector alone will help the economy to develop quality human capital in near future to face WTO challenges.

REFERENCES

1. Books

a. Hassan Rangriz & Abbas Haji Karimi, (2004) *Human Resource Productivity in the Globalised World*, Abhijeet Publications, Delhi.

b. Howard, Richard S., (2000), *Understanding the Global Economy*, Maadhyam Book Services, Delhi.

c. Verghese N.V. (1992), *Technical Changes and Human Resource Development—Issues in human capital Theory*, (Ed.) Kothari V. N., Himalaya Pub. House, Bombay, pp. 187-197.

2. Journals/ Periodicals/ Reports:

a. Deodhar, S.Y., "Educational Services—Issues for India in WTO Negotiations", *Economic and Political Weekly*, Vol. 38, No. 19 May 11-17-2002, pp. 1791-95.

b. Mithilesh Kumar Singh, "Challenges of Globlaisation on Indian Higher Education", *University News*, Vol. 44 No.19, May 8-14, 2006. pp. 1-9.

c. Nigvekar, Arun, "GATS and Higher Education : What is at stake for India", an article appeared in a UGC sponsered seminar, S.N.D.T. University, Mumbai, May, 2002.

d. Paul, Gibs, "Higher Education as a market: a problem or solution?", *Studies in Higher Education*, March - 2001, pp. 85-94.

e. Sausi, Mary and R. Seetharam, "Global Challenges and National Response", *University News*, Vol. 44, No. 33, Aug. 14-20, 2006. pp. 12-18.

f. Susheela Subramanayam, "Globalization: Challenges and opportunities", *Southern Economist,* Vol. 41, No. 12, Oct. 15, 2002.

g. Mannivannan, D.G. (2006) "The implication of GATS trade in HE services: The Indian perspective of private participation", *University News,* Special issue, pp. 127-136.

h. National Knowledge Commission Report, 2006.

7

WORLD TRADE ORGANIZATION & INDIAN AGRICULTURE: AN UNFINISHED AGENDA

*Sudhakar Dwivedi & Arun Bhadauria**

Introduction

Though agriculture continues to be the main stream of Indian economy, yet its contribution in total export of the country is not very encouraging. After the introduction of economic reforms in the country the situation has changed altogether. It is widely accepted that in the initial face of economic reforms manufacturing sector received a greater weightage as compared to agricultural sector. The things were not so serious till agriculture was not brought on the main agenda of World Trade Organization (WTO). It was because of two reasons. Firstly, the import intensity of agriculture sector was not so high and secondly, this sector was considered to be less significant for the purpose of earning foreign exchange. However, after the establishment of WTO the issues pertaining to agricultural sector in general and agricultural exports in particular have drawn the attention of both researchers and policy-makers. It is significant to note that the agenda on agriculture of WTO has great bearance upon the agriculture production of developing countries including India. It is the fact, which has drawn the attention of policy-makers to take

* Faculty members, DDU Institute of Rural Development, B.R. Ambedkar University, Agra, U.P.

suitable policy measures for safeguarding the interest of Indian farmers. Not only that but this is also very important in the context of raising overall growth rate to the tune of 8 per cent or more as targeted in subsequent Five Year Plans (FYP), for which it is necessary to raise growth rate in agricultural sector to the level of over 4 per cent.

Agriculture in post WTO era has become strategically important for India. Besides, it's traditional importance; it can be a potential foreign exchange earner. But it all depends on the fact, how well we can reap the benefits of WTO regime. The WTO agreement on agriculture is stipulated to bring agriculture effectively for the first time under the discipline of the multilateral system. The trading arrangements evolved by WTO are a judicious mix of indicated, suggested and restricted measures. The agreement on agriculture under WTO has far reaching effects on Indian agriculture. The basic objectives of this agreement were to initiate substantial progressive reduction in support and protection resulting in reforms in world agriculture trade so as to make it more purposive and more transparent. Besides solving the traditional problems of Indian agriculture, it has to be made more competitive in the liberalized trading system. There is therefore, a need to inject the elements of productivity and efficiency in agriculture production. Unless we do this, we cannot prepare ourselves to reap the advantages of liberalized trading system. It is this fact, which has put agriculture on the centre stage of policy and planning framework.

In the ninth FYP document, agriculture growth occupied the highest priority. The objectives of reducing the incidence of poverty and removal of unemployment were sought to attain primarily through accelerated agriculture growth. The focus has however, shifted from growth in agriculture to sustainable development of agriculture. An emphasis has been made to increase the rate of gross value addition in agriculture and making its terms of trade favorable. Similarly the approach paper of tenth FYP lays greater emphasis on agriculture production. While there has been greater emphasis on enhancing the productivity of agriculture at domestic front, efforts are also being made to create exportable surplus in agriculture. According to Ninth FYP 16.68 million tones of food grains and 4.25 million tones of oilseeds, 123.5 million kg of tea and 220 million kg of coffee were the targets for creation of exportable surplus in the plan period. Greater emphasis has been laid on those areas, which have great potentials for exportable surplus production and globally competitive[1].

The subject on agriculture export in WTO era has emerged as a matter of concern for both researchers and policy-makers in India and elsewhere. There have been mind-boggling discussions and political parlays on the issue, for what should be the Indian line of action in New International Economic Environment. There is a unanimous view of all concerned that adequate policy measures are the first and foremost requirement so as to make Indian agriculture globally competitive. India has been a founder member of WTO and leading signatory to all the important agreements including on agriculture under WTO. There is no way to step backward. It is therefore of paramount interest to analyze the issues relating to agriculture exports of India under WTO. It is significant to note that agro-food production constitutes a large share in agriculture production. It is also considered to be a potential foreign exchange earner for the country. Therefore, the study of agro-food exports of India could be of vital interest to planners and policy-makers.

The bugbear that had engulfed Indian psyche on account of rising intervention of WTO regulations has now seems to be subsiding. This attributes to the fact that Indian economy has been sailing quite smoothly through the crossroads of promising imbibitions of growth in economic activities and expanding service sector and successful to raise its million's voice to account its claim to be self-reliant. With the start of 2005, the panic of subjugation under the threat of World Trade Organization's (WTO's) agreements have disappeared as ministerial conference of Singapore has failed to break the deadlock between two sections of traders and no guess can work that what way should it adopt. However, it is high time to learn lessons to survive future-crisis as have experienced in yesteryears. For instance it will be worth-thinking that Globalization is here to stay. The hypotheses and scapegoats of unidentified dangers either have proved wrong or have disappeared from the scene. At this juncture, it would not be wise to talk about the false-hood of swadesi. The issue now is what form Globalization should take whether encourages the expansion of international trade and investment. The most convincing fact is that WTO would hold the cradle for the future international trade and we have to find the way most feasible for working in WTO era. Under the purview of WTO, Agreement on Agriculture (AoA), Multi-Fibre Agreement (MFA), Trade Related Intellectual Property Rights (TRIPs) and Trade Related Investment Measures (TRIMs) has emerged one of the most controversial and challenging issues, which have remain main cause of confrontation between member states at many occasions and in which member countries are extremely polarized. The challenges facing the South Asian region due to the process of globalization and its implications for the agriculture sector are enormous characterized by high trade distortions and protections. We must celebrate our success in attracting the attention of developed countries towards the unity of developing countries.

But we should not forget that developing countries are not strong enough in front of developed countries. We must initiate the process of shaping our future strategy to fight the boomerang. We need to assess how much is at stake for us in agriculture. Does it matter if developed countries become reluctant to negotiate further and adopt their imperialistic style of dealing with developing or third world countries?

This paper is an effort to analyze the opening of new avenues in agriculture exports in WTO era. The part-I of the paper critically examines the WTO agenda of agriculture reforms in the first decade of new millennium. This paper also takes full account of India's trade relations with rest of the world during last few years. Part-II discusses trends of Agricultural Exports with trade blocs and other Less Developed Countries (LDCs). Part-III put need to harness vast potential of Agro-Food Export from India in post Cancun. Next part analyzes the emerging prospects of multilateralism over bilateralism or vice-versa. Concluding part of it explores possibilities of new tie-ups with other countries under the aegis of Free Trade Areas and WTO regime

PART-I

Cancun: A Great Divide?

The fifth Ministerial Conference of the 146 members WTO held at Cancun in Mexico was supposed to carry forward the negotiations put in the Doha Ministerial meet and set the tone for the future events. Though it could not make any stride in the contentious issues pertaining to the developing countries especially India, Brazil etc. Moreover it failed to negotiate even on those issues that were supposed to be settled before January 2005. Needless to mention that the launch of the Doha Development Agenda negotiations gave a big boost to the multilateral trading system and it was important that Cancun should have delivered on the promises that were built into the Doha negotiations. The Meet could not develop consensus amongst its members. This all happened due to the fact that Cancun Ministerial Conference turned out to be a ministerial of alliances for the developing world. The G-17 (group of developing countries formed to support on the issues pertaining to agriculture) became G-21 and finally emerged as G-22 including India, China, Brazil and South Africa. Meanwhile several other groups also formed following the same line of making blocs[7]. Nevertheless, the Cancun brought about an attitudinal change in the developed countries for the developing world as they were caught unaware with the level of preparedness and unity of their developing counterparts. However, need of the hour is to look into the matter. Does it matter if developed countries become reluctant to negotiate further and adopt their imperialistic style of dealing with developing or third world countries? India would analyze its trade prospects with ASEAN, SAARC and all the other trade blocs. Thus the Cancun Ministerial can be termed as a 'Great Divide'.

India and other constituents of G-22 would welcome the WTO for being the main avenue to provide necessary framework to facilitate multilateral trade. The rule of WTO is mandatory in order to ensure success of multilateralism over regionalism and bilateralism[3]. But the emergence of trading blocs during the Cancun Meet is a sign of conflict that may persist. In this context India would have to follow the policy of wait and watch as to encash positive repercussions, if any, as it has been in the form of Business Process Outsourcing (BPO). In the mean time India must assess its potential in all the sectors in general and agri-business in particular.

PART-II

Future Prospects of India's Agri-Business with Rest of the World

Trends of Agricultural Exports with Major Trade Blocs

Inception of WTO in 1995 opened the floodgates to the global trade. Overnight countries had to devise suitable strategy to negotiate with the incoming flow of crossroads from all corners. All of them who were part of GATT automatically turned to be members of WTO. Those who weren't part of any such forum/bloc has felt great difficulty to devise suitable trade related strategy. Nevertheless they were also ignorant about their most traded commodities and did not know where their potential lies most. India, however was the member of GATT and have decided to join the WTO quite obviously, has never thought before seriously about most traded commodities and their potential which could be utilized to find its place in the global trade.

India had been trading with almost all the big/small countries of the world. Agricultural exports had a vital place in India's trade relations. Initially we were quite comfortable with whatever, we were exporting. But soon with the opening of floodgates, we realized that this could not be sustained for long unless we do not improve quality of our product and take a big leap in food processing industry. Moreover, rapid growth of Agro-Food based exports by south East Asian countries in food processing and other agricultural-allied activities forced India to think about its own potential. Debate over the usefulness of Agri-Business became centre of all discussions and negotiations nation-wide and later on of course internationally. The realization of its hidden potential was apparently a good sign of change in our approach.

Agreement on Agriculture (AoA) under the aegis of WTO charter opens up debate on various modalities of exports of agricultural products. Market access, tariffication and protection have found special mention in the draft of AoA. As per the modalities shown in the draft, developing countries find it very difficult to trade with rest of the world freely. This draft clearly refutes theory of multilateralism and tries to establish the idea of Most Favoured Nation (MFN) and Non Tariff Barriers (NTBs). Consequently, countries like India involved themselves as a part in the formation of various trade ambitious groups such as G-22, G-33 and G-15 etc. At this juncture it is quite appropriate to work out trends of trade with all the major and minor trade blocs and even with those who are not the part of any blocs. India would also have to analyze its trade prospects with ASEAN, SAARC and all the other trade blocs. This is appearing from the fact that terms of trade are not improving with ASEAN and volumes of export have drastically reduced over the period of few years. As contrary to it terms of trade have improved quite fabulously with OECD. This is however to be noticed significantly that no improvement in total export has been seen even in case of OECD. But as far as NAFTA is concerned both terms of trade and volume of exports have shown noticeably favorable signals. Terms of trade with SAARC nations have appeared favorable but these figures do not have any significance for Agri-Business in India until it has separate trade bloc. Moreover, figures of trade with SAARC do not reveal complete fact about the trade in agro-food products. If we look at product wise export data, we find that almost same number of commodities is being exported to every bloc. This certainly approves idea of multilateral trade relations. However, to observe the trade efficiency it was desirable to observe the trend of exports to major trade blocs in last few years, especially after 1998-99. This would present a good picture of impact of WTO after the said year signifying transitional year.

Keeping this in mind, Analysis of the trade relations and performance of India's exports with different countries and trade blocs over few years is desirable. The data reveals that terms of trade are most favourable with SAARC and NAFTA while terms of trade are favourable with OECD and EU except ASEAN. However the data for Exports with the same blocs for the year 2000-03 unveils surprising fact that indices of exports are in favorable direction with ASEAN and some countries from SAARC. Terms of trade have improved quite fabulously with OECD but no improvement in total export can be seen with the same. But as far as NAFTA is concerned both terms of trade and volume of exports have shown favorable signals (Table 1). Terms of trade with SAARC nations have appeared favorable but these figures do not have any significance for Agri-Business in India. It will become clearer if we have a look at top market destinations for Agro-products throughout the world. OECD provides market for 173.3 percent of major Agro-Products as selected by APEDA. EU (110 %), NAFTA (56.67%) are included in OECD (Table 2). Therefore, India would have to go to world market blocs especially EU, NAFTA and OECD as they happened to be large product destinations for India's Agro-Food products in general and Agro-Processed Food products in particular (See Appendix). Though former Prime Minister Mr. A.B.Vajpayee had envisaged the establishment of free trade blocs SAFTA (see notes) but its constitution is still not clear and has not been proposed yet. Detailed analysis reveals the fact that downward trend with some countries of EU is the outcome of problem of quality and standards, which can be overcome. While with some countries of EU, NAFTA and OECD it was only relative difference not the absolute as the total volume of exports have risen from 0.67 per cent to 0.84 till 2003-04, which have led to the difference in absolute sense. The most appealing fact revealed by this discussions is that trade has received favourable trends from the countries of middle east Asia like Kuwait, UAE and Iran over the few years. Agri-Export Zones (AEZs) for Potato at Agra (Uttar Pradesh, India) have exported most of its potato to UAE (Dubai) while AEZ for Onions and Vegetables in Karnataka and Andhra Pradesh are continuously trading with Sri Lanka.

This may emerged as an separate trade blocs and may be named as West Asia Free Trade Area (WAFTA) or Middle East Free Trade Area (MEFTA).*

Direction of Trade: Countries-Wise, Product-Wise:

To make our discussion more authentic we finally take into the account the performance of India's trade with major countries in the last few years computing indices of exports and imports as well. Discussion with indices of exports revealed that exports to NAFTA are a good deal while with those countries that are not the part of any trade blocs are favourable too. While import indices reveled that EU, OECD and Other countries are the best destination for trade. This clearly states that India will not take the risk to go out of negotiations with countries of NAFTA and would also concentrate upon regional trade. Product-wise India is trading with all countries irrespective to any specific country. Though the type of commodities being traded are of traditional type and not fully processed. This bare fact for instance put future of India's Agri-Business on dark side as India is processing very small volume of its total produce while Malaysia is processing 83 percent. This is why some experts refute the view of Free Trade Area by calling them Flop Trade Agreements[4&5].

Appropriate Stand in WTO Regime for Trade:

For the last four years the whole debate during all the ministerial conferences, other meetings and summits has centered on the various types of subsidies as mentioned in the AoA. These subsidies are meant for extra protection given to the farmers and cultivators to avoid unwanted interference and competition. So far subsidies provided by the Indian Government so far, these do not come under questionable limit as mentioned in AoA. This is however a different but relevant matter that the pattern to raise subsidies is highly questionable in Indian context, which calls for policy makers to review the functional objective behind these subsidies. Subsidies should not be indiscriminately to various odd

---

* Not created, and there is no such plan. This is only a hypothesis.

sections of the community rather they must be devoluted with a view to give incentives to the farmers for their hard work[6]. The basis, character, forms and procedure of providing subsidies at present actually allows a vast opportunity to traders and suppliers to corner sizeable money from public exchequer. Obviously more rationalized and productive subsidies can offer opportunities and avenues for higher earnings and thereby uplifting their quality of life. But such a drastic move requires a very strong political will. This would certainly boost the morale of masses and of course then they would be in position to elect good and efficient public representatives. Around Rs 4000 crores go waste every year just on account of subsidies. Moreover, well-off consumers, middlemen and traders salt this huge sum away. That ultimately causes burden on taxpayers. The system that is not beneficial to any one in real terms, not even to the poor whom it is claimed for.

The trade performance over last few years clearly reveals that exports are not healthy as transaction cost is not favourable. Policy makers recognize that transaction cost is sliding from 19 per cent to 22 per cent on the value of exports[7]. Consequently on the policy front, the ministry flags as urgent the issues of rebating all possible duties, levies and taxes suffered by exporters and making export promotion schemes WTO compatible. Raising concern over the transaction cost one should not forget that tariffs, levies, custom duties are major concern of developing world with developed countries. If we are making our products export compatible, others should counter it. Provided that Non Tariff Barriers and Most Favoured Nation type barriers should not put any hurdle[8]. In case they continue, countries like India would have no option but to find its remedy by keeping all options open to trade with regional blocs.

Domestic and Regional Concerns

There has been complete shift in the policies since the adoption of economic reforms after 1994-95. Agriculture and allied sector are now being considered as potential foreign exchange earner. Earlier less than fifty percent populations were economically active but this number has risen to 61 percent over the last decade. Though we lag far behind than that of China (69 per cent economically active population) but being largest democracy and largest agriculture sector we have huge prospects for Agri-Business in India. Per Agriculture Worker value addition is Rs. 397 while it is as high as Rs 34,727 in USA, Rs. 19930 in Germany and Rs. 28665 in Japan[9]. We must take care of competition with rest of the world in general and South Asian region in particular. We have observed India's trade with major trade blocs all over the world.

If we look at the percentage of Agro-Products processed in the countries in this region then it becomes clear that India has to go long way. In Thailand 30 percent food products are being processed while this is 78 percent in the Philippines and 80 percent in Malaysia. Though Philippines is not the part of SAFTA but this has close bearings upon the trade relations of the countries in this region[10].

PART-III

Need to Harness Vast Potential of Agro-Food Export from India in Post Cancun

The prospects for the trade in this sector are not dull as compared to the other sectors. Government has given it top priority in tenth plan and has estimated that the production of fruits and vegetables and other processed food products would reach 80 percent of the total quantity of food grains produced in India by 2010[11]. The present status of food processing industry though seems to be very minimal as it has very low level of contribution in food processing. These figures do not show the exact and exclusive picture of total food processing potential in India. In fact, India's food processing industry includes large number of Agro-Food product, which comes from agriculture and allied sector. Among these diversified product line several products have shown huge potential of export demand and hence good source of earning foreign exchange. Such products and their sub-sectors are being described here.

1. India exported fruits and vegetables worth Rs. 5240

million in 1997-98. The horticulture production was around 100 million tonnes and FDI stood at nearly Rs. 8000 crores.

2. India's current level of meat and meat-based exports is around Rs. 8000 million. FDI is around Rs 5000 million, which happens to be 50 per cent of total investment in this sector.
3. India ranks fifth in the annual egg production.
4. Milk and milk products performed with 4 per cent growth at the time of worldwide recession (growth rate was –2).
5. FDI in Fisheries was of the order of nearly Rs. 7000 million[12].

Moreover, the processing food industry ranks fifth in size in the country representing 6.3 per cent of GDP. It accounts for 13 percent of the country's exports and 6 per cent of total investment. The estimated size is at US $ 70 million, including 22 billion of value added products[13].

PART-IV

Multilateralism Vs Bilateralism

In the recent past India has enjoyed the expansion of its service sector. India has recorded sound development in Information Technology (IT), BPO-ITES, medical transcription and application software. On the other hand, China has emphasized on the improvement in its manufacturing sector. Though both the countries have largest manpower in the world, but they are nurturing their manpower in the field where they finds comparative advantage. India prefers self-reliance by developing its inner strength and want to least dependent on FDI while China is receiving $ 50 bn FDI every year compared to only $ 4 bn FDI in India[14]. Consequently India does record slow growth but sustained. Indian Economy is developing steadily and will certainly improve its manufacturing sector. However, She has to seek advantage of being agriculture-based economy. If we look through the statistics of export competitiveness of Indian Crop we find that traditional crop seldom appear cost competitive in international market (See notes). While cereal crop are not found cost-competitive, processed food products and edible oils are appearing as most internationally demanded products. This is therefore we must encourage processing of agro foods. We should not forget that despite of being 1 billion, processing insignificantly. However, we are exporting to every major trade blocs. Establishment of Agri-Export Zones have opened new horizons of processing long range of agro-food products like gherkin, strawberry, potato, mango etc. Moreover we have been already doing quite well in several products like milk, meat, onion etc. This is therefore India is on advantage to practice Agri-Business in post-Cancun. India certainly going to have advantage in agri-business provided she adopts a sound strategy and policy framework and planning for the same. In this scenario, India must not forget its identity and previous policies. She has never favoured unilateralism and bilateralism (as indicated from trade relations with major trade blocs) in trade relations. India must develop its infrastructure to support the agri-business and would negotiate for true multilateralism in WTO (see notes). At the same time India would maintain the pace of developing inter-regional trade in South-Asian region, as it will promote its economic, political and social interests.

NOTES

1. Out of total Agro products, APEDA: Agro-Processed Food Products Export Development Authority has selected 30 products for development. APEDA prepares the record of total exports at regular intervals and provide the requisite information.
2. SAFTA: South Asian Free Trade Area (as same as NAFTA), In the Ministerial Meet at Islamabad. Prime Minister Mr. A.B.Vajpayee proposed SAFTA in which member nations would form a trading bloc and would engage themselves in inter-regional trade.
3. Export competitiveness of most of the commodities in India has undergone significant changes during 1990s. At the time of inception of WTO international agricultural prices were moving on a rising trend,

which however showed a decline in trend after 1997. Indian Rice was found competitive throughout while wheat and coarse grains were not found fit. Soya bean is found export competitive. Domestic Resource Cost indicates that wheat and maize are efficient import substitutes[10].

4. Indian Premier Man Mohan Singh has stated at Jakarta that India is standing for all the issues concerned with developing world but it would seek neutral attitude and would welcome true globalization.
5. The Indo-Thai FTA (ITFTA) has been in effect from September 2004. The SAFTA and ITFTA can be compared with regional trade blocs of US (NAFTA) and EU. Amongst FTAs the key issue is whether the economies of the countries entering into an FTA complement or compete with each other[4]. In fact, when these FTAs were signed, there was a commitment from the Government that issues like anomalies in the duty structure would be resolved before the FTAs are implemented.
6. Mr. Rahul Bajaj, Chairmen Bajaj Auto writes in *Times of India* that FTAs are the sign of Global trade and are appearing quite favourable in USA etc. For the successful FTA it is necessary that Member countries should have suitable and soothe climate, which is not found in this region. FTA may not be very promising until our handicaps are removed. The Indo-Thai FTA (ITFTA) has been in effect from September 2004. The SAFTA and ITFTA can be compared with regional trade blocs of US (NAFTA) and EU. Amongst FTAs the key issue is whether the economies of the countries entering into an FTA complement or compete with each other[4]. In fact, when these FTAs were signed, there was a commitment from the Government that issues like anomalies in the duty structure would be resolved before the FTAs are implemented.
7. As per the editorial of *Times of India,* about 20 years ago, then prime minister Rajiv Gandhi reckoned that only about 15 per cent of the money intended as subsidies actually reached the poor[6]. Farmers can be

given food stamps (a kind of food currency) that can be used to buy only specific eatables.

8. According to Ministry of Commerce, India's exports are on a high growth path. But are now faced with huge challenges including poor infrastructure and high transaction cost[8].

9. Commerce and Industry Minister, Mr. Kamal Nath has recently said that Non-Tariff Barriers (NTBs) are cause of concern. The barriers, which are other than health and safety related obviously, driven by commercial interests[7]. Generalized system of Preferences (GSP) will also bother if India is not a part of it.

Sudhakar Dwivedi is presently Senior Faculty at Department of Agriculture Economics, D.D.U. Institute of Rural Development, Agra University, Agra. His area of specialization is Agricultural Marketing and Agricultural Production Economics. He has contributed number of research papers so far to various national and international journals.

Arun Bhadauria is presently guest faculty at Institute of Rural Development, Agra University, Agra. His area of specialization is Agricultural Marketing. He is continuously engaged in research work and has contributed a number of papers and research articles to many research journals of repute.

REFERENCES

1. *Drafts for Ninth and Tenth Plan from Handbook* (2003), Kitab Mahal, New Delhi.
2. Bhargava, Sunil (2003): 'WTO & Cancun Conference', *Journal for Chartered Accountants in India*, New Delhi, Dec.
3. Bhaumik, T.K. (2003): 'WTO, South Asia and Related Issues', *Liberal Times*, vol XI/ no 2, p.p-36-37.
4. Bajaj, Rahul (2005): 'Flop Trade Agreements-Exports need policy impetus, not low tariffs'; *Times of India*, April 28, New Delhi.

5. Bajaj, Rahul (2005): 'Flop Trade Agreements: Exports Need Policy Impetus, Not Low Tariffs'; *Times of India,* New Delhi, April 28, p-14.
6. Editorial (2005): 'Thought for Food: Scrap Subsidies, Top up incomes'; *Times of India,* New Delhi, March 15, p-14.
7. Times News Network (2005): 'Exports buoyant but face bumps ahead'; *Times of India,* New Delhi, June 24, p-18.
8. Nath, Kamal (2005): 'India Warns against dividing developing nations at WTO'; CII Conference; *Times of India,* Tuesday, New Delhi, March 15.
9. Statistical Outline of India (2002), Tata Services Limited, Mumbai.
10. Annual Report (2003): Food Processing Industry in India, www.google.com
11. *Ibid.*
12. Sen, Amitabh (2003): 'Food Processing Industry in India'. Google.com
13. *Ibid.*
14. Jhunjhunwala, B. (2005): 'Success of China: Don't Scared', *Daily Amar Ujala,* April 19.
15. Ramesh Chand, (2001), *Trade Liberalization, WTO and Indian Agriculture-Experiences and Prospects,* Mittal Publications, New Delhi.
16. Bhargava, Sunil (2003): 'WTO & Cancun Conference', *Journal for Chartered Accountants in India,* New Delhi, Dec.
17. Bhaumik, T.K. (2003): 'WTO, South Asia and Related Issues', *Liberal Times,* vol. XI, no. 2, pp. 36-37.
18. Sen, Amitabh (2003): 'Food Processing Industry in India', Google.com.

Table 1: Trade with Major World Blocs

(In US $ Mn)

Trade Blocs	*94-95*		*99-00*		*00-01*	
	Export	*Import*	*Export*	*Import*	*Export*	*Import*
ASEAN	1902	1940	2192	4919	2836	3864
SAARC	1215	177	1396	398	1925	432
EU	7319	7580	9349	10989	10379	10320
NAFTA	5367	3212	9114	4046	10156	3244
OECD	15976	15512	21841	22863	24246	20576
Total*	35396	35973	49382	57816	56241	42495

Source: Statistical Outline of India 2002-03.

* Total of trade from all blocs throughout the world.

List of types of Products:

1. Floriculture-- floriculture (01) and fruit and vegetable seeds (02)
2. Fruits and vegetables-- fresh onions (03), other fresh vegetables (04), walnuts (05), fresh mangoes (06), fresh grapes (07) and other fresh fruits (08).
3. Processed fruits & vegetables—dried & preserved vegetable (09), mango pulp (10), pickles & chutneys (11) and other processed fruits & vegetables (12).
4. Animal Products Foods—buffalo meat (13), sheep/ goat meat (14), poultry products (5), dairy product (16), animal casing (17) and processed meat (18).
5. Other processed Food—groundnut (19), guar gum (20), jaggary & confectionery (21), cocoa product (22), cereal preparation (23), alcoholic beverage (24), miscellaneous preparation (25) and milled product (26).
6. Cereals—basmati rice (27), non-basmati rice (28), wheat (29) and other cereals (30).

Table 2: Percentage of Commodities Marketed in Major Trade Blocs

Major Market Blocs	*Types of Products*	*Percentage Share*
ASEAN	13	43.3
SAARC	21	70
EU	33	110
NAFTA	17	56.67
OECD	52*	173.3

Source: Apeda and List of trade Blocs.

- OECD includes several countries, which are the part of either EU, SAARC, and any other trade blocs and it is true for EU and others. Therefore figures are not exclusive.

List of Product Destinations

Name of Blocs	*Nations*	*Number of Products*
NAFTA	USA	16
	Canada	01
EU	Italy	02
	France	02
	Germany	06
	Belgium	01
	Netherlands	07
	UK	12
	Spain	02
	Portugal	01
ASEAN	Indonesia	03
	Singapore	02
	Korea Rep	01
	Malaysia	04
	Hong Kong	02
	China	01
OECD	EU	33
	NAFTA	17
	Australia	--
	Japan	02
SAARC	Sri Lanka	09
	Bhutan	--
	Pakistan	02
	Nepal	01
	Maldives	--
	Bangladesh	09

Table 2: List of Product Destinations

Name of Blocs	*Nations*	*Number of Products*
NAFTA	USA	28
	Canada	28
EU	France	27
	Spain	25
	Germany	27
	Netherlands	27
	Belgium	25
	U.K.	28
	Italy	24
	Portugal	19
ASEAN	Indonesia	27
	Singapore	27
	Malaysia	27
	China	29
	Hong Kong	28
	Korea	26
OECD	EU	29
	NAFTA	28
	Australia	27
	Japan	26
SAARC	Pakistan	19
	Bhutan	9
	Sri lanka	28
	Nepal	29
	Bangladesh	26
	Maldives	25

Source: APEDA.

Table 3: Direction of India's Trade with Various Countries Throughout World

Name of Country	*Percentage Contribution*					
	Exports			*Imports*		
	1999-2000	*2000-2001*	*Index*	*1999-2000*	*2000-2001*	*Index*
USA (NAFTA)	22.7	22.8	100.44	7.7	5.5	71.43
Germany (EU)	4.8	4.3	89.58	4.0	3.3	82.50
Other European Union (EU)	14.3	13.2	92.31	12.1	8.9	73.55
UK (EU)	6.0	5.4	90.0	5.8	6.4	110.34
Japan (OECD)	4.5	4.3	95.55	5.0	4.3	86.0
Russia	2.5	2.1	84.0	1.3	1.1	84.6
OPEC	10.6	10.5	99.05	23.8	6.0	25.21
Other East EU (EU)	0.5	0.4	80.0	0.4	0.5	125
Asia (ASEAN & SAARC)	20.4	20.1	98.52	17.5	13.7	78.21
Other Less Developed Countries	4.8	5.1	106.25	5.0	4.0	80.0
Others	8.9	11.8	132.58	7.7	46.3	601.29

Source: Economic Analysis 2000-2001, Ministry of Finance, GOI.

Table 4: Comparative Analysis of Trade with Major Trade Blocs

Countries	*Trade Blocs*	*No. of products exported to*	*Value of exports (Lakh Rs) (2000-01, 2001-02, 2002-03)*	*% to the total exports*
Pakistan	SAFTA*	19	21303.849	2.31
			10069.347	0.99
			3312.608	0.24
Bhutan	-do-	9	·76.079	0.008
			1132.061	0.11
			3127.175	0.23
Sri lanka	-do-	28	27046.492	2.94
			28887.713	2.84
			28334.363	2.05
Nepal	-do-	29	4974.520	0.54
			5589.287	0.55
			9161.388	0.66

Bangladesh	-do-	26	77177.371	8.38
			105901.059	10.41
			149728.740	10.83
Maldives	-do-	25	3037.00	0.33
			3032.00	0.30
			3208.00	0.23
France	EU	27	12671.121	1.38
			9293.281	0.91
			12877.946	0.93
Spain	-do-	25	6852.296	0.74
			6823.240	0.67
			7762.849	0.56
Germany	-do-	27	18211.785	1.98
			14984.548	1.47
			21576.353	1.56
Netherlands	-do-	27	18541.71	2.01
			15558.77	1.53
			17421.77	1.26
Belgium	-do-	25	8203.170	0.89
			7648.783	0.75
			9249.105	0.67
U.K.	-do-	28	55616.285	6.04
			42526.451	4.18
			46731.200	3.38
Italy	-do-	24	6381.554	0.69
			6470.007	0.64
			5701.934	0.41
Portugal	-do-	19	965.00	0.11
			649.00	0.16
			922.31	0.07
U.S.A	NAFTA	28	77077.884	8.37
			60841.168	5.98
			90419.109	6.54
Canada	-do-	28	9499.811	1.03
			8263.042	0.81
			10043.899	0.73
Indonesia	ASEAN	27	23295.0	2.53
			37422.19	3.68
			90369.27	6.54
Singapore	-do-	27	9543.53	1.04

			15143.00	1.49
			18129.02	1.31
Malaysia	-do-	27	57827.442	6.28
			71186.363	6.99
			102102.201	7.38
China	-do-	29	4403.00	0.48
			8078.19	0.79
			8808.97	0.64
Hong Kong	-do-	28	3324.71	0.36
			4033.25	0.39
			2782.20	0.20
Korea	-do-	26	13429.31	1.46
			10541.00	1.04
			11609.53	0.84
Japan	OECD	26	7912.564	0.86
			8912.671	0.88
			9822.212	0.71
Australia	-do-	27	4686.110	0.51
			4991.153	0.46
			5943.174	0.43
Kuwait	WAFTA**	28	32793.035	3.56
			29343.826	2.89
			27947.578	2.02
U.A.E.	-do-	28	73082.938	7.93
			75801.656	7.45
			78675.726	5.69
Iran	-do-	19	6139.523	0.66
			8169.408	0.80
			5494.046	0.40

Source: DGCIS, Annual Volume, apeda.com.

*Proposed to constitute by 2006.

**May be created.

8

FOREIGN DIRECT INVESTMENT IS A BREAKFAST FOR FASTING INDIA

*R. Hiremani Naik**

1. Introduction

India's economic policy reforms have played a critical role in the performance of the Indian economy since 1991. Among other things, the reforms have involved opening the economy, making it more competitive, getting the government out of the huge legacy of regulation, empowering the states to take more responsibility for economic management and thereby creating a kind of competition between the states for foreign investors. The GDP growth rate, which had collapsed to 0.8% in 1991-92 rebounded to a near normal 5.3% in 1992-93, and then accelerated to 6.2% in 1993-94. Subsequently, the GDP grew at an average rate of 7.5% in the three years 1994-95 to 1996-97, before slowing down to 5.1% in 1997-98. It is important to note that despite the slowdown, the average growth rate in the four years 1994-95 to 1997-98 was 6.9%, significantly higher than the growth rate of 5.6% achieved in the 1980s. In 2005-06, the GDP is estimated increased in a drastic manner and reached to 9.1 percent.

In terms of foreign investment, it is the direct investment that should be actively sought for and door should be thrown wide open to Foreign Direct Investment (FDI). FDI brings huge advantages such as new capital, technology, managerial

* Reader, Department of Commerce, Karnatak University, KRC PG Centre, Belgaum-Karnataka State.

expertise, and access to foreign markets with little or no downside. Many international investors would flock to India right now as they found India as a safety zone in comparison with China. However, they are put off by the fact of poor availability of infrastructural facilities in India.

Foreign Direct Investment is an important form of foreign capital, which has become crucial in the world economy. In this circumstances, it is necessary to make conceptual framework of FDI is of utmost importance before discussing any ramifications of FDI. FDI refers to investment in a foreign country where the investors retains control over it. However, the extent of control varies from 10% to 100%. If typically takes the form of starting a subsidiary, acquiring a stake in the existing firm or starting a joint venture in the foreign country. Normally, investment and management of the firm concerned go together and both the guest and the host countries have long-term interest in FDI.

2. What is FDI?

According to International Guidelines based on the recommendations by IMF in its balance of payment manual, FDI is defined as "International Investment that reflects the objective of a resident entity in one economy (foreign direct investor or parent enterprise) obtaining a 'lasting interest' and control in an enterprise resident in an economy other than that of the foreign direct investor". Lasting interest implies the existence of a long-term relationship between a direct investor and the enterprise and a significant degree of influence on the management of the enterprise. The general rule of thumb presented in the manual is that the direct investor owns (or control) at least 10% of the ordinary shares, voting power or equivalent. Therefore, FDI flows are the sum of three basic components viz, equity capital, reinvested earning and other capital associated with various inter-company debt transactions. In case of India, RBI and Secretarial furnish FDI Statistics Industrial Approvals (SIA). However, the definition and computation of FDI used by RBI do not conform to the guidelines of the IMF. Thus, RBI definition is not consistent with IMF as a result of which there is considerable under valuation of FDI flows to India.

3. FDI under Industrial Policy

The Government's liberalisation and economic reforms programme aims at rapid and substantial economic growth, and integration with the global economy in a harmonised manner. The industrial policy reforms have reduced the industrial licensing requirements, removed restrictions on investment and expansion, and facilitated easy access to foreign technology and foreign direct investment. All industrial undertakings are exempt from obtaining an industrial licence to manufacture, except for :

a) Industries reserved for the Public Sector,
b) Industries retained under compulsory licensing,
c) Items of manufacture reserved for the small scale sector

India has several advantages like availability of natural resource the entrepreneurship, access to the sea coast and a vast labour force as like coastal China except the interest of Government which neglected this for a long time. It, even today, overlooks the role of industrial facilities, infrastructure, land area, and effective port facilities that one needs to be able to compete with China in this area. But it is here, where one could find tens of millions of jobs over the next few years in real, significant foreign exchange earning private sector activity.

4. Major Impediments to Larger FDI Inflows in India

In addition to India's poor performance in terms of competitiveness, quality of infrastructure, and skills and productivity of labour, several other factors make India a far less attractive ground for direct investment than the potential she has. Given that India has a huge domestic market and a fast growing one, there is every reason to believe that with continued reforms that improve institutions and economic policies, and thereby create an environment conducive for private investment and economic growth that substantially large volumes of FDI will flow to India. Some of the major deterrents are as follows :

a) The FDI regime in India is still quite restrictive. Consequently, we regard to cross border venture. Foreign ownership of between 51 and 100 percent of equity still required a long procedure of governmental approval.

b) Expeditious translation of approved FDI into actual investment would require more transparent policies and a drastic reduction in time-consuming red-tapism.

c) India's tariff rates are still among the highest in the world, and continue to block India's attractiveness as an export platform for labour-intensive manufacturing production.

d) The reform process so far has mainly concentrated at the central level. India has yet to free up its state governments sufficiently so that they can add much greater dynamism to the reforms.

e) The very modest contributions of India's export processing zones to attracting FDI and overall export development call for a revision of policy. India's export processing zones have lacked dynamism because of several reasons, such as their relatively limited scale; the Government's general ambivalence about attracting FDI; the unclear and changing incentive packages attacked to the zones; and the power of the central government in the regulation of the zones, in comparison with the major responsibility of local and provincial government in China.

f) While the reforms implemented so far have helped remove the entry barriers, the liberalization of exit barriers has yet to take place. This is a major deterrent to large volumes of FDI flowing to India. An exit policy needs to be formulated such that firms can enter and exit freely from the market.

g) Large firms in India are not allowed to retrench or layoff any workers, or close down the unit without the permission of the state government. While the law was enacted with a view to monitor unfair retrenchment and layoff, in effect it has turned out to be a provision for job security in privately owned large firms.

h) A Reform of India's financial sector is crucial for large FDI flows into India. However, only some partial steps have been undertaken and these are by no means going to make any meaningful changes to the existing system.

i) High corporate tax rate is definitely a major disincentive to foreign corporate investment in India with respect to tax evasion.

5. Extent of FDI in India

Policies in the post-reform period have emphasized upon greater encouragement and mobilization of non-debt creating private capital inflows for reducing reliance on debt flows. Since then there has been increasing inflows of foreign investment in the country in terms of FDI investment. Further, in respect of selected Asian Economies indicate that 14% of total Global FDI inflows accounted by Asian Economies alone. India, though well behind China in attracting FDI inflows, it has marginally improved its share in total FDI inflows from 2.7% in 1996 to 3.3% in 2001. This sharp increase in volume during 2001 underlines the importance of India as an Investment destination. Liberalization of the FDI policy regime has resulted in a substantial expansion of FDI approvals and flows. The total number of foreign collaboration approvals from January 1991 to march 2004 is 11,546. Out of the total approvals, 38.93 per cent is comprised by electrical equipments sectors, 9.54 percent by services sector, 9.12 percent by chemicals, 6.95 by telecommunication, 6.68 percent by food and food processing sector, 6.07 per cent by energy and the rest is comprised by textile, metallurgical industries and hotel and tourism. FDI is permitted through financial collaborations, joint ventures and technical collaborations, capital markets via Euro issues and private placements or preferential allotments. FDI is not permitted in industrial sectors like Arms and Ammunition, Atomic Energy, Railway Transport, Coal & Lignite & Mining of Iron, Manganese, Chrome, Gypsum, Sulphur, Gold, Diamonds, Copper, Zinc.

Foreign Investment through GDRs is treated as Foreign Direct Investment Indian companies are allowed to raise equity capital in the international market through the issue of Global Depository Receipt (GDRs). GDRs are designed in dollars and are not subject to any ceilings on investment. An applicant company seeking Government's approval in this regard should have consistent track record for good performance (financial or otherwise) for a minimum period of 3 years. This condition would be relaxed for infrastructure projects such as power generation, telecommunication, petroleum exploration and refining, ports, airports and roads.

6. Procedure for Approval

Foreign Direct Investment (FDI) is now recognized as an important driver of growth in the country. Government is making all efforts to attract and facilitate FDI and investment from Non-Resident (NRIs) including Overseas Corporate Bodies (OCBs) that are predominantly owned by them, to complement and supplement domestic investment. To make the investment in India attractive, investment and returns on them are freely repatriable, except where the approval is subject to specific conditions such as lock in period on original investment, dividend cap, foreign exchange neutrality, etc. as per the notified sectoral policy. Foreign direct investment is freely allowed in all sectors including the services sector, except a few sectors where the existing and notified sectoral policy does not permit FDI beyond the ceiling.

FDI for virtually all items/activities can be brought in through the Automatic Route under powers delegated to the Reserve Bank of India (RBI), and for the remaining items/activities through Government approval. Government approvals are accorded on the recommendation of the Foreign Investment Promotion Board (FIPB).

Automatic Route

a) New Ventures

All items/activities for FDI/NRI/OCB investment upto 100% fall under the automatic route. Whenever any investor chooses to make an application to the FIPB and not to avail of the automatic route, he or she may do so. Investment in public sector units as also for EOU/EPZ/EHTP/STP units would also qualify for the automatic route. Investment under the automatic route shall continue to be governed by the notified sectoral policy and equity caps and RBI will ensure compliance of the same.

b) Existing Companies

Besides new companies, automatic route for FDI/NRI/OCB investment is also available to the existing companies proposing to induct foreign equity. For existing companies with an expansion programme, the additional requirements are that,

i. Increase in equity level must result from the expansion of the equity base of the existing company without the acquisition of existing shares by NRI/OCB/foreign investors.

ii. Money to be remitted should be in foreign currency and;

iii. Proposed expansion programme should be in the sector(s) under automatic route.

For existing companies without an expansion programme, the additional requirements for eligibility for automatic approval are that:

i. They are engaged in the industries under automatic route,

ii. The increase in equity level must be from expansion of the equity base.

iii. The foreign equity must be in foreign currency.

The automatic route for FDI and/or technology collaboration would not be available to those who have or had any previous joint venture or technology transfer/trade mark agreement in the same or allied field in India. Equity participation by international financial institutions such as ADB, IFC, CDC, DEG, etc. in domestic companies is permitted through automatic route subject to SEBI/RBI regulations and sector specific cap on FDI. In a major drive to simplify procedures for foreign direct investment under the automatic route, RBI has given permission to Indian Companies to accept investment under this route without obtaining prior approval from RBI. Investors are required to notify the Regional Office concerned of the RBI of receipt of inward remittances within 30 days of such receipt and file required documentation within 30 days of issue of shares to Foreign Investors. This facility is available to NRI/OCB investment also.

Actual investments are made in a phased manner depending upon business needs. In terms of the country-wise breakup of FDI inflows in terms India extending to it the special tax relief and the inflows routed through Mauritius. It may be seen that Telecom, Electrical Equipment including Computers, Energy and Transportation are the key sectors which account for 50% of the total FDI inflows.

Government Approval

Government approval for FDI/NRI/OCB through the FIPB shall be necessary for various categories, which are mentioned as follows:

a. Proposals that require an Industrial Licence which includes (1) the item requiring an Industrial Licence under the IDR Act, 1951;
b. Foreign investment being more than 24 per cent in the equity capital of units manufacturing items reserved for small scale industries; and
c. Items which require an Industrial Licence in terms of the location policy notified by Government under the New Industrial Policy of 1991.
d. Proposals falling outside notified sectoral policy/caps or under sectors in which FDI is not permitted.
e. Areas / sectors / activities hitherto not open to FDI/ NRI/OCB investment shall continue to be so unless otherwise decided and notified by Government.

7. Investment Risks in India

Following are the Important Investment Risks in India:

a) Sovereign Risk

Sovereign Risk in India is therefore zero for both "Foreign Direct Investment" and "Foreign Portfolio Investment".

b) Political Risk

India suffered political instability for a few years due to the failure of any party to win an absolute majority in Parliament. Thus, political instability in India, in practical terms, posed no risk to foreign direct investors because no policy framed by the past government has been reversed by any successive government so far.

c) Commercial Risk

Commercial risk exists in business in any country. There is a large number of market research firms in India which study demand/supply situation for any product/service and advise the potential investor accordingly in exchange of a professional fee.

d) Risk of Foreign Sanctions

India did not seem to be in the good books of the United States government due to its nuclear weapons and missiles development policy. The threat of foreign sanctions is therefore of academic and speculative value.

e) Unmentioned Pitfalls

i. Since the launch of "Manmohanomics" by the Narasimha Rao Government in 1991—FDI has been touted as the magic wand that will transform "Under-developed" India into an advanced nation with a "modern" infrastructure. However, is FDI—truly the panacea for the ills of the Indian economy ?

ii. Majority of FDI has come in the form of speculative investments in India's stock market, where select scripts have seen phenomenal jumps in their stock prices, while stocks of some major Indian manufacturing companies have languished at very low valuations.

iii. Power Shortages : Contrary to the view that power

shortages emanate from a lack of generating plants, it revealed from a detailed investigation that the main problem appears to be poor efficiency of existing plants. Recently, during a conference on power generation, it was stated that if India could check the leakages of boiler tubes, 5,000mw of additional electricity could be generated. In addition the power transmission and distribution losses in India are very high. None has taken the crucial decisions required to solve the power crisis.

iv. The Emerging Telecom Scandal : When the Indian government opened up cellular telephony to private industry – several foreign investors lined up to enter India's telecom sector. A process of competitive bidding led to licensing agreements that required telecom operators to pay license fees in exchange for connectivity to the fixed-line network that had already been set-up by the Department of Telecom (DOT) and MTNL—the telephone provider in Delhi and Bombay.

8. Conclusion

Though the FDI inflows into India have shot up over the past decade, it is still very lesser than other developing countries. There are lot of opportunities for investments in various sectors of Indian economy as it has been facing the shortage of capital and technology for growth and developments. Hence, the Government of India should try to attract more and more FDI by adopting good governance practices on par with international standards instead of borrowing to invest in various sectors and to meet trade deficits by incurring liability of regular interest payment and repayment of principles on time. The government has to take the benefit out of the LPG by inviting FDI in those fields where it actually needs as a breakfast for fasting sector.

REFERENCES

1. Lucas, R.E.B. on the Determinants of Direct Foreign Investment Evidence from East and South East Asia World 1993, p213.
2. R. Nagaraj : FDI in India in the government's : Trends and Issues, *EPW*, April 26, 2003, p. 41.
3. Government of India : Indian Economic Survey Planning Commission, Government of India 2002, 2003, 2004 and 2005.
4. Kumar, N.: *Multinational Enterprises in India*, Routledge, London-1990.
5. World Council for Corporate Governance, Recommendations of the IInd Corporate Governance Council February 2002, p45.

9

WTO AND ITS IMPACT ON SMALL SCALE INDUSTRIES

K. A. Rasure

Introduction

Small-Scale Industries (SSIs) have acquired a prominent place in shaping the economy of India since Independence. Historically, SSIs have had a special place in developmental policy by generating employment, production and income through widely dispersed sectors across different geographical locations of our country. Today, they account for almost 40 per cent of the total industrial production, about 80 per cent of industrial employment and 35 per cent of exports of India (GoI, 2001; Naik, 2002). In addition, they account for about 95 per cent of all industrial units, which provide employment to 186.8 lakh people spread over 34 lakh units all over the country. Thus, SSIs have a major role to play in accomplishing the potential national export target of US $80.5 billions in 2006-07 (Narayan, 2002).

Small-scale industries over a wide range of products (8,000), which include modern and traditional sectors. Of which, 836 items of 1045 products account for 13 per cent which are reserved (Hussain, 1997). Of late, the total number of items reserved for SSIs have come down to 674 in India's

* Reader in Economics, Nrupatunga Arts, Commerce, Management and Science College, SEDAM - 585222. District Gulbarga (Karnataka)

budget of 2003-04 (GoI, 2003). In contrast to this, the number of items on the Open General License (OGL) have increased from 478 during 1998-99 to 714 during 2001-02. However, in spite of special patronage by both Central and State governments, SSIs have remained mostly tiny, traditional and lack the competitive spirit (Ayyar, 1994; GoI, 1997). SSIs survive in India due to product and geographical market segmentation and policy protection. In the era of liberalisation and globalisation, this role of segmentation and government protection is getting reduced (Tendulkar and Bhavani, 1997). In short, government policies on SSIs clearly bring out the shift from 'protection-led growth' to 'competition-led growth'.

At the national level, there has been a steady increase in the growth of production in the SSI sector which peaked in 1995-96 at 11.4 per cent from 3.1 per cent in 1991-92 and thereafter declined to 8.43 per cent in 1997-98 and to 8.1 per cent in 2000-01 (Singh, 2001).

On the export front, the growth shows a worsening trend. It registered a growth of 17.7 per cent in 1995-96 from 43.7 per cent during 1991-92. It fell to 2.7 per cent in 1998-99 and recovered to 5 per cent in 2000-01. As far as employment is concerned, SSIs accounted for 3.6 per cent of the total industrial employment in 1991-92, increased tp 4.1 per cent in 1995-96, fell to 2.6 per cent in 1998-99 and again increased to 4 per cent in 2000-01 (GoI, 2001). Unfortunately, in the recent past, the Indian economy has been facing several external and internal shocks, whose impact is seen in the fall of growth of employment, production and exports, of SSIs in particular, and industry in general. An external shock includes the East Asian crisis of 1997-98 and oil price increase of 2000-01. Internal shocks comprise natural disasters and consecutive years of poor agricultural performance due to monsoon failures. Added to these, the global economy has been going through an overall depression, which has been reflected in an output growth of 2.4 per cent for the past few years. Despite the above, SSIs registered a higher growth rate than the entire industrial sector during 2002-03. In general, they account for 3.8 per cent of unit growth 7.5 per cent of production and 3.9 per cent of employment (GoI, 2002).

Need for the Study

The World Trade Organisation (WTO) regulates multilateral trade agreements of its member countries, disciplines import quotas and other import restrictions, reduces import tariffs, and insists on removal of subsidies and concessions for export of domestic goods by 2003 (Kumar, 2000). This has opened up competition from foreign industries (particularly after withdrawal of government protection) with the import of quality goods from the advanced countries and inexpensive goods from other developing countries. In this context, though this sector shows substantial progress in terms of its contribution to the economy, it is important to know how SSIs in India are coping with the present new challenges being posed to them. Further, it is essential to gauge the future scenario of SSIs and determine policy alternatives for dealing with problems.

Objectives of the Study

With the above background, the specific objectives formulated for the present study are : *(a)* to assess the awareness of WTO and its agreements among small-scale industrialists; *(b)* to analyse the performance of SSIs. Keeping in view these objectives, the paper is organised as follows: First, an introductory note is provided, next, a brief overview of the WTO is provided, followed by the general implications of WTO agreements on SSIs. Finally, the remedial measures and prospects are discussed, conclusions and the implications of the study are presented.

WTO : An Overview

WTO is global international organization dealing with the rules and regulations of trade between member nations. The core of WTO is in its framework agreements and negotiations, which are signed and legally approved by the 145 members (WTO, 2003). The main objective behind these agreements and negotiations is support to producers of goods and services, intellectual property rights, exports and imports (Bhalla, 1996). Historically, the base of WTO lies in the General Agreement of Tariffs and Trade (GATT). The WTO, the successor to GATT, is rapidly establishing itself as the third pillar of the Bretton Woods Institutions alongside the International Monetary Fund (IMF) and the World Bank (International Bank for Reconstruction and Development) which were established in July 1944. Interestingly, India was one of the 23 founder members. Due to resistance from the US Senate, the International Trade Organisation (ITO) could not be established along with the other two institutions, which came into existence on December 27, 1945. However, in its place a protocol of provisional applications (GATT) was signed on January 1, 1948. GATT was only a multilateral adhoc body to provide rules for world trade from 1948 to 1994. The Uruguay Round, the 8th round of talks under GATT during 1986 to 1994, led to the birth of the WTO on January 1, 1995 (Bhandari, 2002). India is a founder-member of this organization. Today, GATT is the WTOs principal rulebook for trade in goods and services. In addition, the Uruguary Round created new rules for dealing with trade in services, relevant aspects of intellectural property rights, dispute settlement and trade policy reviews. The complete set of WTO agreements and negotiations run to some 30,000 pages consisting of about 60 agreements and separate schedules made by individual members in specific areas such as lowering of customs duty rates and market-opening for services (WTO, 2002).

WTO has underlined six fundamentals, namely, club of nations, free trade among countries, non-restrictive trade with some exceptions, tariffs based on bound rates after negotiations, dismantling of non-tariff barriers and all countries to be accorded Most Favoured Nation (MFN) status (Gupta, 2000). In general, it is a regulatory body of world trade to ensure free, transparent and predictable trading regimes in the world. In addition, WTO monitors compliance by member countries with a number of agreements, which collectively govern multiple dimensions of trade relationship among member countries. Further, it acts as a dispute settlement body over conflicts arising from actions taken by countries in violation of agreements, Therefore, all the member countries are bound to honour their commitments to different trade agreements under the WTO. However, the crucial question relating to WTO is what sort of trade regime it seeks to promote and to what extent the new discipline can safeguard the export interests of member countries.

General Implications of WTO on SSIs

Implications of WTO and its agreements on SSIs are not different from its implications to industry in general because they comprise the major part of Indian industry, As mentioned above, SSIs contribute about 54 per cent of non-traditional and 10 per cent of traditional product exports (taken together about 35 per cent of total exports of our country). However, SSIs have to face threats and also avail opportunities owing to WTO and its agreements. The main opportunities of the WTO are: *(a)* national treatment (or MFN) for exportable items all over the world with better market access through Internet; *(b)* enlightened entrepreneurs have greater opportunities to benefit from their comparative advantages due to lowering of tariffs and dismantling of other restrictions; *(c)* industries that are in constant touch with Government, which in turn negotiates the best of their interests in the on-going dialogue with WTO, are going to benefit (Laghu Udyog, 2003). However, India has a real chance of becoming a superpower is service sector, particularly IT. It has already captured about 25 per cent of world exports.

On the other hand, the negative effects are the following: *(i)* SSIs have to face competition by way of cheap imports from different countries due to the removal of Quantitative Restrictions (QRs) on imports and lowering of tariffs. As a result, every single individual enterprise, small or big, whether exporting or serving the domestic market, has to face competition. *(ii)* OGL opens up the possibility of direct competition in the domestic market with the imports of high quality goods from developed countries and cheap products from other less developed countries (Bhavani, 2002). Subsequently, entry of multinational companies intensifies competition in the domestic market. However, Indian SSIs are not in a position to compete with others due to in-built weaknesses like poor quality, costly credit, weak infrastructure, traditional technology, inflexible labour laws, lack of information and international exposure, and ineffective associations. *(iii)* Export market will become tougher because of competition among developing countries with similar comparative advantages.

In the view of the above, WTO agreements suggest ways by which some of the adverse consequences could be neutralized. These are the use of Agreement on Trade-Related Aspects of Intellectual Property Rights (TRIPS), Agreement on Trade-Related Investment Measures (TRIMS), and stringent hygienic, environmental and labour standards. In addition, these agreements themselves provide for certain in-built safety mechanisms like anti-dumping, countervailing and safeguard measures. Further, strict vigilance at the ports of entry is required to ensure that imported goods are as per quality standards are invoiced and carry the name of the manufacturer and maximum retail price (WTO, 1998b). Interestingly, WTO prohibits subsidies, which directly affect price competition of the product. However, it helps activities of common interest, which act as an indirect way of subsidy to the enterprise.

Table 1: Performance of Small-Scale Industries

Year	*Units (in Lakh)*	*Production (Rs. Crore)*	*Employment (in Lakh)*	*SSI Exports (Rs. Crore)*
1994-95	79.6	1,22,210	191.4	29,068
1995-96	82.8	1,48,290	197.9	36,470
1996-97	86.2	1,68,413	205.9	39,248
1997-98	89.7	1,89,178	213.2	44,442
1998-99	93.4	2,12,901	220.6	48,979
1999-2000	97.2	2,34,255	229.1	54,200
2000-2001	101.1	2,61,289	239.1	69,797
2001-02	105.2	2,82,270	249.1	71,244
2002-03	109.5	3,11,993	260.1	86,013
2003-04	114.0	3,51,427	271.4	NA

Source: RBI, Hand Book of Statistics on the Indian Economy 2003-04.

Industrial Development—The Basic Philosophy

The goals and objectives set out for the nation on the eve of independence, namely, the rapid agricultural and industrial development of our country, rapid expansion of opportunities for gainful employment, progressive reduction of social and economic disparities, removal of poverty and attainment of self-reliance, remain as valid today as at the time when Pandit Jawaharlal Nehru first set them out before the nation. Any industrial policy must contribute to the realization of these goals and objectives at an accelerated pace. The present statement of industrial policy is inspired by these very concerns, and represents a renewed initiative towards consolidating the gains of national reconstruction at this crucial stage.

Policy Initiatives

Industrial policies over the years have promoted SSIs through various incentives in order to fulfill socio-economic objectives. These incentives related to financial, fiscal and infrastructural measures and were targeted at achieving the growth of the sector during the various Plan periods. Incentives were extended either on a "one time" basis (initial support for setting up units) or in the form of sustained support for a specific period (protectionist measures, subsidies, etc). While some incentives were made applicable to all industrial units including the large-scale sector, others were available exclusively for the SSIs.

Industrial Policy Resolution, 1948 spelt out the details of some basic and strategic industries to be established by the State in addition to those, in which the private sector could be permitted to play a role, subject to controls and regulations. The policy aimed at balanced growth of different manufacturing sectors and focused on the co-existence of large, cottage and small industries. An emphasis was laid on the promotion of cottage and small-scale industries as these could play a crucial role in the rehabilitation of displaced persons through the establishment of individual/cooperative enterprises.

Industrial Policy Resolution, 1956 supported the initiation of measures to improve the competitive strength of the small enterprises while recognizing the role of SSI sector in providing employment opportunities, mobilizing local skills and capital resources, and integration with the large sector.

Emphasis was placed on the creation of facilities such as industrial Estates and rural community workshops to provide the required production technologies, other amenities and incentives.

Industrial Policy Statement, 1977 stressed the wider dispersal of cottage and small industries into rural areas and small towns. It emphasized that "whatever could be produced by small and cottage industries must only be so produced". This led to the expansion of the list of reserved items for exclusive production by the SSI sector. The concept of the Tiny Sector was introduced giving special consideration and extending help by way of provision for margin money assistance. The concept of District Industries Centers (DICs) was also mooted so that in each district a single agency could meet all the requirements of village and small industries under one roof.

Industrial Policy Statement, 1980 focused on integrated industrial development and suggested the setting up of nucleus plants in these districts, which were identified as industrially backward with the expectation that these would help the spatial dispersal of small ancillary units and the existing network of SSI units would grow faster. SSI units were redefined by raising the ceiling of investment in plant and machinery.

Industrial Policy, 1990 introduced important measures like raising the investment ceilings in plant and machinery for SSIs, export oriented and tiny units, creating a central investment subsidy exclusively for the SSI sector in rural and backward areas, assisting women entrepreneurs with an objective of widening the entrepreneurial base.

Industrial Policy, 1991 announced "New Policy Measures for Small, Tiny and Village enterprises" with the objective of imparting a vitality and growth impetus to the sector. These measures were announced subsequent to the policy of delicensing, decontrol deregulation, overall liberalization and structural reform of the economy in general and industrial and trade policies in particular that were initiated in July 1991. Small-Scale and ancillary undertakings were exempted from licensing for all articles of manufacture, which were not covered by the reserved list for Public Sector, and those kept under compulsory licensing. The investment limit for tiny enterprises was raised to Rs. 0.5 million and locational conditions were withdrawn. All industry related service and business enterprises (with an investment ceiling as those of tiny enterprises) irrespective of location, were recognized as SSIs. Equity participation by other industrial undertakings was permitted up to a limit of 24 per cent of shareholding in SSIs to boost ancillarisation and a strengthening of the capital base. A new scheme of Integrated Infrastructural Development (including technological backup services) for SSI was provided for with the participation of state governments and financial institutions.

Remedial Measures

- More Industrial/Technology parks with all facilities for small industries will be established.
- Quality will be uppermost concern in customer-oriented economy. Acquiring ISO 9000 and other standards will be crucial.
- Rapid Technological obsolensce exerts tremendous pressure on SSI to upgrade/modify/process technologies.
- Small units will be environments friendly and necessary certifications will have to be obtained.
- Access to global markets, tie-up with foreign partners for import of technology and buy-backs.
- Preferential treatment in allotment of infrastructure facilities, setting ups of mini-industrial units and cluster industries.
- Greater weightage to tiny units will continue.
- Co-operative arrangements between units manufacturing the same products will consolidate the negotiating power in the market will not be far.
- Making available integrated (Composite) term loan for higher amounts on preferential terms.
- Collateral guarantee from institutions will boost the establishment of tiny and small-scale units.

- Credit rating institutions will play a prominent role in acting as intermediaries and arranging of loans etc.

Prospects and Outlook

- The process of liberalization, while providing tremendous opportunities, has thrown up new challenges for the Indian small scale industries sector.
- For SSIs, the globalization of economic activities has two interfaces. For some, the process opens new opportunities to expand and grow, for others, a much larger group the process is a threat from abroad.
- In view of the important of SSI sector and to provide a further impetus to its contribution in the overall economy, a new Ministry for Small Scale Industries and Agro Rural Industries has been created.
- With regard to the definition of Small Scale Industry, a school of thought has propagated the introduction of new concept of Small and Medium Enterprises in Indian context. This would be in line with the concept of SMEs prevalent the world over.
- In view of emerging WTO regime and a high-level reservation redundancy, there may be a need to reconsider orienting of the existing Government policies so as to achieve a phased dereservation of 812 reserved items.

Conclusion

The main focus of this paper is to assess the awareness, growth and performance of SSI units and identify the factors contributing to sales turnover. The study has found the following : *(a)* Entrepreneurs are experiencing the implications of WTO and its agreements by classifications ; however, awareness about WTO agreements and its implications is poor. *(b)* Entrepreneurs are not satisfied with the existing infrastructure availability. *(c)* Growth rates of output, domestic sales, exports and imports are positive for most of the units but inconsistent among categories.

To compete successfully with internal or/and external industries, SSIs should use quality raw materials improve productivity, and reduce costs. To do this, the study suggests that Government : *(a)* review its and its agreements and also motivate them to face the new challenges; *(b)* provide good infrastructure and technology upgradation; as required *(c)* take necessary action for prompt payments by medium– and large scale industries and provide timely and adequate credit; *(d)* invite foreign investment for better technology transfer and improve the skills of labourers; *(e)* arrange marketing support for, encourage diversified export base, and promote role of associations and non-government organizations in setting up of common facilities in technology, marketing, infrastructure and other support services through private and public partnership, rather than provide subsidies.

Appendix 1 : Important WTO Agreements

Sl.No.	*Agreement*
A	Marrakesh Agreement establishing the World Trade Organisation
B	Multiateral agreements
1	Trade in goods
	1.1. General Agreement on Tariffs and Trade (GATT)
	1.2. Agreement on Implementation of Article VII of GATT
	1.3. Agreement on Pre-shipment Inspection (PSI)
	1.4. Agreement on Technical Barriers to Trade (TBT)
	1.5. Agreement on Application of Sanitary and Phytosanitary Measures (SPM)
	1.6. Agreement on Licensing Procedures
	1.7. Agreement on Safeguards
	1.8. Agreement on Subsidies and Countervailing Measures (SCM)
	1.9. Agreement on Implementation of Article VI of GATT (Anti dumping)
	1.10. Agreement on Trade-Related Investment Measures (TRIMs)
	1.11. Agreement on Textiles and Clothing (ATC)
	1.12. Agreement on Agriculture
	1.13. Agreement on Rules on Origin
2	Trade in services
	2.1 General Agreement on Trade in Services (GATS)
3	Intellectual Property Rights (IPRs)
	3.1 Agreement on Trade-Related Aspects of Intellectual Property Rights (TRIPS)

C	Plurilateral trade agreements
	C.1. Agreement on Trade in Civil Aircraft's
	C.2. Agreement on Government Procurement
	C.3. International Dairy Agreement
	C.4. International Bovine Meat Agreement

Source: www.wto.org.

REFERENCES

- Ayyar, S.R.S (1994). New Emerging Challenges and Opportunities for Small and Medium Enterprises through Technological Upgradation and better Financial Management; *Small Industry Bulletin for Asia and Pacific,* No. 29, p.38-40.
- Bhalla, A.S. (1996). *Facing the Technological Challenge,* London, Macmillan Press.
- Bhandari, S. (2002). *World Trade Organisation and Developing Countries,* New Delhi, Deep and Deep.
- Bhavani, T.A. (2002). Small-Scale Units in the Era of Globalisation : Problems and Prospects, *Economic and Political Weekly,* 37 (29), pp. 3041-3052.
- D. Pandurang Rao, *WTO & Competitiveness,* Excel Books.
- Francis Cherunilam, *Business Environment,* Himalaya Publishing House
- GoI (1997). Government of India, Ninth Five-Year Plan 1997-2002, Planning Commission, New Delhi, 2, pp.609-614.
- GoI (2001). Government of India, *Economic Survey 2001-2002,* Ministry of Finance and Company Affairs, Economic Division, New Delhi, pp. 180-182.
- GoI (2002). Government of India, *Economic Survey 2002-2003,* Ministry of Finance and Company Affairs, Economic Division, New Delhi, pp.151-152.
- Gupta, K.R. (2000). *World Trade Organization,* Delhi, Atlantic Distributors and Publishers, Vol (1).
- Hussain, A. (1997) Report of the Expert Committee on Small Enterprises, Ministry of Industry Department of Small Scale Industries and Agro and Rural Industries Government of India, New Delhi; pp.182.
- Kumar, A. (2000), WTO Agreements: Its Impact on Small Scale Sector, *Laghu Udyog Samachar,* 24 (6-8), pp. 28-39.
- Laghu Udyog (2003). www. Laghu-udyog.com, WTO: An Overview and the Agreements, accessed on April 1.

- *Laghu Udyog Smachar,* a journal of small scale industries.
- Naik, S.D. (2002). Small Scale Industries : preparing for the WTO challenges, *The Hindu Business Line,* Chennai, July 12, p.6
- Narayan, M.R. (2002). Big Package for Small Industries, Economy and Business : *Deccan Herald,* Bangalore, 4 March, p. 11.
- Singh, M.P. (2001). Small Scale Sector and Union Budget 2001-02, *Laghu Udyog Samachar,* 25 (5-8): 17.
- Tendulkar, S.D. and T.A. Bhavani (1997). Policy of Modern Small Scale Industries : A Case of Government Failure, *Indian Economic Review,* 32 (1), pp. 39-64.
- WTO (1998b). *Trade Policy Review: India,* Geneva, World Trade Organisation.
- WTO (2002). http://www.wto.org, What is the WTO, accessed on August 31.
- WTO (2003). http://www.wto.org, Fact File, accessed on February 18.

10

INDIA AND WTO—A VIEW ON GLOBALISATION AND AGRICULTURE AGREEMENT

*A. Bose * & A. Marimuthu ***

The term 'globalisation' has been commonly referred since the 1990s to reflect technological advances that have made it quicker to carry out international transaction—both trading and financial flows. Moreover, economic 'globalisation' refers to the increasing integration of economies around the world, particularly through trade and finance (*The Economist*, 7th March 1995). The term sometimes also refers to the movement of people and technology across international borders. Broader cultural, political and environmental dimensions of globalisation arte not discussed rather the study is aimed at policies related to certain institutions.

Globalisation rests on the argument that we are experiencing quantitatively and qualitatively different levels of international integration in the area of finance and production. In the realm of finance, it is argued that unprecedented international expansion and linkages—global financial deepening—are overriding the possibilities for national financial economic management. Cornia argues: "States have lost the power to use range of financial controls

* Lecturer, Department of Commerce, Govt Arts College, Melur, Madurai – 625 106.

** Lecturer, Department of Economics, R.D. Govt. Arts College, Sivagangai – 630 561.

and policy instruments to shape and promote economic development. Transformation of finance, however, has taken a more widespread and structurally complex form in the late 20th century" (Cornia, 1999 : 18).

Globalisation embodies integration of international markets for goods, finances, services, but certainly not labout. Despite the success in the East Asian economies, most of the developing countries are part of the international division of labour, where these economies are integrated in the global market as a subordinate to the interest of the developed countries (Bagchi, 1992). It relies on the process of structural change, which has critical implications for growth, equity and poverty in the developing counties. In the context, trade liberalisation policies are measures to stimulate structural change by reorganising production through more reliance on market forces rather than state, forging closer interaction between the national and global economy

The World Bank and IMF's policies on economic reforms are based on the "neo-liberal" or "market-friendly" policy that is intellectually predominant over the past two decades and more. It seems that the globalisation is the result of the rich countries imposing trade deals and other accords to the poor countries thus making it easier for corporations to dominate the economies of the poor nations around the world without having obligations to the peoples of those nations (Stiglitz, 2002; Sen, 1999; Strange, 1992).

Neoliberalism and Globalisation

Neo-liberal polices are supposed to play a key role in globalisation. In recent years, agencies like World Bank and IMF have been active proponents of globalisation and rapid integration of developing economies into the world markets through increased production for markets and trade, foreign investments and capital mobility (World Bank, 2002).

Neo-liberalism has been the dominant global economic trend adopted by the Washington consensus and these initiatives are characterised by free market policies to encourage private enterprise and consumer choice rewarding entrepreneurial initiative. As a result, policies are invoked to rationalise things from lowering taxes on the rich, scrapping environmental regulations, dismantling public education and social welfare programmes. The economic consequences of these policies in Latin America, South Asia and Africa has been of a massive increase in social and economic inequality, a marked increase in deprivation for poor, a disastrous environment, and an unstable global economy. It is claimed that the spoils of the growth and wealth will invariably spread to the broad mass of the population (Deation and losers as production becomes more concentrated in a more integrated world. The technical changes have rendered globalisation inevitable. However, 'neo-liberal globalisation' has unleashed an unequal world order that is unsustainable.

'Neo-liberal globalisation, its logic and consequences, participants and the success story' (Morley, 1994; Roy, 1993) analyses attracting foreign capital and investments thus raising productivity especially for developing countries where about 4 billion people live in poverty, is important to understand (Cornia, 1999). Various studies carried out on these issue suggest that East Asia and Latin America, especially the former, in contrast to Africa, are emerging as more competitive in international economy thus providing base to expend trade and business (World Bank, 2002; Singh, 1993).

Moreover, globalisation and openness is not new, as being portrayed. The history of capitalism since the very beginning has been the history of western expansion and the system was always global. It is incorrect to say that globalisation is totally new. After all what was the colonisation of India, Sri Lanka, Indonesia, Malaysia, Philippines, Algeria, Angola, Kenya, Nigeria, Senegal, South Africa, Zambia, Jamaica, Cuba, and many more countries, which today are known as developing countries, if not globalisation? The colonisation of Americas since 16th Century was globalisation. It has never been achieved by peaceful and equal negotiations between peoples. The conventional integrations between peoples. The conventional growth theorist would argue that accelerated integration of the poor economies into the world economies would create larger markets for the poor countries products. And ultimately they would have better opportunity to grow and catch up with the rich countries. Globalisation, Nayyar (1997), for example, uses/it in positive sense to denote the increased international integration of trade, investment and finance. However, in the late-19th Century many developing countries were integrated in the world market in terms of international trade, finance, and foreign direct investments. It is only during the interwar period that the highly global economy became inward looking and the process was halted (Siddiqui, 1990a). However, after the Second World War, barriers to trade, investment and financial flows were slowly dismantled despite that many developing countries were sceptical and reluctant to participate initially (Singer and Roy, 1993).

The political economy of South Asia during the period of late 1980s and early 1990s changed dramatically. By the late 1980s Cold War was coming to an end with the collapse of Socialist bloc. The opposition between capitalist and socialist countries disappeared. Transformative pressures led to a wave of liberalisation in South Asian countries. India adopted the policy of economic liberalisation in 1991, while the country had severe balance of payment crisis (Bagchi, 1994).

Economic Growth and the Question of Poverty

Economic growth is considered to be an important factor in reducing poverty and inequality in developing countries. Some economists find strong correlation between gross domestic product per capita and indicators of development such as life expectancy, poverty and infant mortality. The data shows that the world economy has grown about five fold since 1950s, an unprecedented rate of increase. However, the developed countries still dominate economic activity, accounting for $ 22.5 trillion of the $ 27.7 trillion global GDP in 1995. Nevertheless, a remarkable trend over the last two decades has been the role played by the South Asian economies.

So what is the link between globalisation and poverty? Globalisation involves: production and trade, finance and capital flows and labout. On Globalisation vs. trade and production, Watkins (2002) observes: "Openness—along with associated free market reforms—holds the key to making globalisation work for the poor .... International trade has the potential to act as a powerful catalyst for poverty reduction, as the experience of East Asia demonstrates. It can provide poor countries and people with access to the markets, technologies, and ideas needed to sustain higher and more equitable patterns of growth... But if 'globaphilla'—an affliction, widespread on Nineteenth Street in Washington, that holds that increased integration through trade and openness, is an almost automatic passport to rapid growth and poverty reduction" (Watkins, 200:1).

The 20th century witnessed unprecedented economic growth; with global per capita GDP increased almost five fold. But this growth was not steady. As Figure 1 a divides the century into four periods. During the inter-war period, the trade was minimal and countries retreated into closed economies, protectionism and capital controls. Due to a number of factors per capita income growth fell to less then 1% during 1913-1915. However, during the post-World Was boom the per capita income growth over 2% was experienced in the developed countries (World Economic Outlook, IMF, May 2000). That the income gap between high-income and low-income counties has grown wider is a matter for concern and a large number of people continue to live in abject poverty.

India's concerns with World Trade Organization (WTO) are more or less similar to other developing countries, which have for long followed a substantively inward looking policy. In India, a vast agriculture sector and public sector dominated service economy, which have made the process of liberalization at the behest of WTO both politically dangerous and economically costly. The major areas of concern for India are:

1. The success of maintainability of Quantitative Restrictions on imports and exports.
2. Opening of agriculture and service sectors.
3. Intellectual Property Rights.
4. GATT agreements on agriculture
5. Anti-Dumping and Subsidy Measures.
6. New forms of Non-tariff Measures, such as environment and social clauses.

Quantitative Restrictions (QRs) Regime

According to WTO, all trade restrictions are to be carried out by tariffs. Direct controls through licensing will not be normally allowed (Art XI), except under special circumstances. An important exception is the Balance of Payments ground under Art XII where QRs might be justified in the face of a BOP crisis. Developing countries are allowed a further flexibility under Art XVIII: B. India has maintained QRs on some consumer goods and agriculture product imports. This has been challenged by several trade partners, including USA.

India could negotiate a timetable with most of the countries for the removal of QRs within a span of six years. However, it was not accepted by USA which took India to the WTO Dispute Settlement Panel (DSP) which partially ruled against India and asked USA and India to negotiate for their removal within an acceptable time limit. However, in the 2005-06 import policy, India has removed a large number of items from the quantitative restrictions. Therefore, it can be expected that WTO–mandated liberalization of imports need not be a great danger. Further, it must be remembered that OR removal does not mean free import; the tariffs continue to be imposed.

Opening of Agriculture & Service

Nowadays, agriculture, both in the developed and developing countries is run strictly on business lines. In India, however, it is mostly subsistence agriculture, especially for food crops. India is also largely dependent on agriculture for both visible and invisible absorption of labour. There is a possibility that Indian agriculture may get swamped by giant, international grain merchandising firms, especially in commodities such as wheat where India is not globally competitive.

Similarly, the Indian food security may get adversely affected if faced with cheaper imported grains; Indian farmers change their crop pattern and opt for more cash crops. This can make the country import dependent for food and make it politically vulnerable. However, India has set ceiling rates for agricultural products at sufficiently high levels; 100 per cent for primary products, processed food products at 150 per cent and edible oils at 300 percent. The current applied rates are much lower. Therefore, there is a safety cushion. Wherever for historical reasons, the bound rates are at very low levels, renegotiations of tariff bindings have been sought under Art – XXVIII of GATT.

Indian Patents Act

This Act has been amended to make it consistent with the WTO requirements. Initially, though USA has expressed reservations, it has finally announced that it would not take India to DSB on this. But, in future, further changes would be required under Art. 65.4 of the TRIPs Agreement. The first change may be relating to a uniform patent protection of 20 years for all. Secondly, Art. 28 provides importation as a right of the pattern holder. Finally, under Art. 27, the fields of technology to be patented would have to be defined. This Article provides that inventions for all fields of technology (product and process) would have to be granted patent rights, except

i. Diagnostic, therapeutic and surgical methods for the treatment of human or animals.
ii. Plant and animals other than micro-organisms:
iii. Essentially biological processes for the production of plants and animals other than non-biological and micro-biological processes.

Suppose a country excludes plant varieties from patentability, it is expected to provide protection under a "sui generis" system. Future contentious issues to be resolved are the definition of micro-organisms, the finalization of the Plant Varieties Bill under the sui generis system and the issue of geographical appellation.

GATT Agreements on Agriculture

Generally, agriculture prices are subject to free play of market forces. The domestic agricultural policies both in the developed and developing countries, are directed to intervene in the free play of market forces through input subsidies, support prices, export and import controls, etc. According to GATT, 1994, such policy interventions obstruct international trade in agricultural products.

The GATT, 1994 agricultural package relates to commitments which member countries have to make in respect of market access, domestic support, and export competition.

Tariffication

The GATT agreement on agriculture requires member countries to revise existing non-tariff restrictions such as quotas in agricultural imports by such "tariffs" as would provide substantially the same level of protection. This is called "tariffication" of agricultural trade policy.

Tariff Reduction

Each member has to commit to reduce tariffs resulting from "tariffication" process as well as other tariffs on agricultural products. Developed countries have to lower down tariffs on agricultural products by an average 36 percent in six years from 1995. Developing countries have to reduce tariffs on agricultural produces on an average by 24 percent over ten years from 1995. The most undeveloped countries are not required to make any commitment for reduction of tariffs on agricultural products.

Agricultural Subsidies

The basic aim of GATT, 1994 agreement on government assistance or subsidies given to agriculture is to reduce subsidies which have a bearing on international trade in primary and processed agricultural products. Hence, it specifies the types of agricultural subsidies which are not required to be reduced and those which are required to be reduced by member countries.

Exempted "Green Box" Subsidies

Agricultural support assistance or subsidies having minimum effect on trade are excluded from any member nation's commitment for subsidy reduction. These are called "green box" policies and include:

International Trade

- Assistance for research.
- Assistance for disease control and infrastructural development.
- Direct payment to waste management and environment protection.
- Assistance for "for security" such as food subsidy given under Public Distribution System (PDS) in India. (Maintaining PDS)

However, it is important to note that "food security" assistance or food aid is exempted from a member nation's commitment for subsidy reduction only when it is based on clearly defined criteria related to "nutritional" objectives.

The PDS as it operates in India fails to satisfy the above condition for exempting the "food security" subsidy because both in urban and rural areas, families of the middle and upper income groups constitute a sizable proporation of the PDS beneficiaries. Hence under GATT, 1994, some member nations may object to the food subsidy given in India unless our PDS is overhauled to exclude the non-poor beneficiaries. However, both the union and the majority of state governments are unwilling to introduce this change, mainly on the pretext of practical difficulties.

Non-exempted Agricultural Subsidies

a. Affiliated member countries have to make commitment that they will reduce during the GATT implementation period (1994-1999) the types of government assistance or subsidies to agriculture which are not in the form of "green box" policies. The non-exempted types of subsidies which are required to be reduced include the following:

- Assistance in the form of production-limiting subsidies.
- Assistance given for growth of agriculture and rural development, i.e., procurement at support prices and subsidies on inputs and credit.

b. The above types of non-exempted assistance and subsidies to agriculture are required to be reduced only if their total amount as proportion of value of total agricultural production exceeds 5 percent in case of DCs and 10 percent in case of LDCs. Above these permissible upper limits, the non-exempted subsidies are required to be reduced to be reduced to the extent of 20 percent by developed countries and 13.3 percent by less developed countries before 1999.

Agricultural Exports Subsidy

i. Agricultural Direct Export Subsidy is required to be reduced by 36 percent for DCs and by 24 percent for LDCs in the next five years in order to enhance competition in trade in agricultural products.
ii. Moreover, the overall quantity of subsidized export have to be reduced to 21 percent over the next six years (1994-1999).

Anti-Dumping & Anti-subsidy

The legal provisions relating to these are in Article VI of GATT and the two agreements, viz., the WTO Agreement of implementation of Article VI of GATT 1994 (Anti-Dumping Agreement) and Articles VI, XVI of GATT and Agreement of Subsidies and Countervailing Measures (Subsidies Agreement). The strict adherence of procedural regime relating to these has resulted in large scale utilisation of these policy measures both by the developed and developing countries. India has been one of the worst affected, especially because USA, uses these instruments extensively. Indian Industry is not sufficiently organized to fight antidumping cases abroad which are bot time-consuming and expensive. Since the USP of most Indian exports in low price, the increased use of anti-dumping duty is a matter of grave concern.

Environment, TBT (Technical Barriers to Trade) Stationary and Physiosanitary Measures (SPS)

As per agreement of TBT, SPS is based on fundamental and national treatment. These agreements have threatened a significant proportion of export of India to developed countries.

Environment, as a new issue, has entered the work agenda of WTO. Environmental trade restrictions are becoming common. But India has been affected by some such restrictions. Thus WTO allows some restrictions on environment ground. Under multilateral Environmental Agreements, there are some trades restricting measures. India has some confusion regarding the legitimacy of these restrictions and the inter-se relationship between MEAs and WTO provisions So it is duty of the committee on Trade Environment of deal with these issues.

Benefits of India

The World Trade Organization is an international organization that supervises the rules by which sovereign independent nations trade with each other. The rules are framed through consensus by negotiations between member countries. Memberships of WTO impose certain obligations on all the countries but it also provides protection against unfair practices, particularly from the richer countries. In the absence of international rules of the game, the developing countries like India would be at the mercy of the rich developed countries. Being a member of WTO, India would secure many concession, as China has recently made to the USA and to Europe so as to gain their approval for its membership. India need not fear that foreign investors will swamp the Indian economy and dominate it; this fear is misplaced and creates deleterious atmosphere not desirable to India at this stage. This negative attitude leads to isolationist mentality which ultimately denies India's young people the opportunity to grow to higher levels and also make India realise a honorable position in the world commerce and finance.

New Role for WTO

There is no simple answer to these new agendas. Indeed, it is questionable if the WTO is a suitable forum to negotiate on them in detail. However, so long as a relatively effective governing body on world trade relations has no counterpart in comparably effective instruments to deal with the social and ecological impacts of globalisation, there will probably be repeated attempts to assign new competences to the WTO. Even when it would make more sense not to leave multilateral rules on environmental protection on securing human rights to a trade organisation. That nothing should block the objectives of sustainable development or safeguarding human rights, which go beyond trade policy, must thereby be beyond doubt.

Conclusion

Globalisation and WTO are playing a significant role in growth, poverty and inequality as a result of business and financial liberalisation. Hence it is expected that there will be a decline in inequality and poverty. India lagged far behind China by five years, because China challenges the poverty and inequality and their policy, land reforms, participation in WTO and government measures and actions. Therefore India should also follow China in this respect instead of seeing poverty and inequality of other countries. Self-development should be considered first and then we can think of other countries. It is hoped that India will march ahead by its active participations in WTO negotiations for all-round development in her largest economy at least in future days.

India has many fears and concerns to overcome particularly relating to agriculture, industry etc. Developed countries, it is feared, are likely to exploit developing countries by adopting QRs, income support mechanism, heavy subsidies to farmers, no-tariff walls etc. But the developing countries require protection against these policies as their implementation will result in destitution of farmers, conversion of owner farmers into labourers on their own farms. Developing countries do not at present have competitive ability to face such market situation. India should exhibit confidence and courage to face world markets on its own strength for which WTO is providing Opportunities.

REFERENCES

1. Dr. V. Balu (2001), *International Trade,* pp. 365-367
2. Damodaran (2001), "WTO Agriculture Agreement, Common Property Resources and Income diversification strategy", *Economic and Political Weekly,* September 22, p. 3633.
3. See Nitya Nanda (2004), "WIPO Patent Agenda", *Economic and Political Weekly,* September 25, pp. 4310- 14.
4. Dr. K.N. Ramanujam (2005), "WTO in Indian Context", *Indian Economic Panorama,* pp. 30-31.
5. K.M. Naidu, R. Sanjeeva Rao and K. Manjusree (2006), "WTO and India – A Critical Review", *Southern Economist,* pp. 18 – 19.
6. Batra, G.S. and Dangwal, R.C. (2000), *Globalization and Liberalization: New Developments,* New Delhi : Deep and Deep Publications Pvt. Ltd.,
7. Gupta, Suman *et. al.* (eds.) (2003), *India in the Age of Globalization : Contemporary Discourses and Text,* New Delhi : Nehru Memorial Museum and Library.
8. Guha, Swapna Banerjee (2004), *Space, Society and Geography,* Jaipur : Rawat Publication.

11

SOUTH ASIA TRADE IN THE ERA OF ECONOMIC REFORMS: WITH SPECIAL REFERENCE TO INDIA

*K. A. Rasure**

Abstract

After initiation of economic reforms during the year 1991-92 India emerged as one of the fastest growing economy of the world. The rules of the WTO, signed in 1994, cover trade areas such as food, environmental standards, Regulation of services such as transport, how Government can use taxes, copyright, patent law, Agricultural Policy and more. It has to review the trade Related Aspects of Intellectual Property Rights (TRIPS) and Anti-dumping Practices. Further it is concentrating on additional issues like Foreign Direct Investment, Competition Policy, Environmental Safety, Health and labour standards. Reflecting the regions recent economic reforms, South Asian Economies fared well since 1996, with most countries achieving healthy GDP and export growth rates, improved creditworthiness indicators and increased foreign investment.

The period of nineties is synonymous with reforms for all the members countries. Withdrawal of quantitative

* Dept. of Economics, Nrupatunga Arts, Commerce, Science & Management College, SEDAM – 585222, Dist. Gulbarga (Karnataka) – India

restrictions slashing down of tariffs, dismantling of licensing system and various trade facilitation measures have marked the era of reform. For the four big partners of the group namely Bangladesh, India, Pakistan and Sri Lanka the reduction in average tariff rate has been commendable during the period. For Bangladesh average tariff rate was more than 80% per cent in 1991. In 2001 it stood at just 20 per cent. Pakistan showed a decline from 70% to slightly less than 20 percent. SriLankan tariff rate was quite low at a little above 20 per cent in 1991 which came down to 5 per cent in 2001. This decline in average tariff rate signified easing of restriction on trade and higher market access as well. Since lower tariff rate was applied to the entire world in a non-discriminating manner the impact was felt on the aggregate volume of trade. Thus proportion of trade in GDP was was 24 per cent in 1985-87 for Bangladesh and it reached 35.5 per cent in 2000-01. During the same period the increase was from 61.5 per cent to 89 per cent in the case of Bhutan, from 14 per cent to 30 per cent in the case of India, from 60 per cent to 169 per cent in the case of Maldives, from 32 per cent to 55 per cent in the case of Nepal, from 34 per cent to 36 per cent in the case of Pakistan and from 62 per cent to 85 per cent in the case of Sri Lanka. The country that benefited least from reform seems to be Pakistan while the maximum benefit went to Maldives. Bangladesh and India shared benefit in a modest manner.

The paper is organized into four sections. The first section explains briefly the South Asia Trade in WTO, the second section discusses GATT – WTO and the Indian reform process, and section third focuses on the WTO issues for India, last section comments on the WTO and India's External Sector. The paper heavily depends upon secondary data.

Introduction

After initiation of economic reforms during the year 1991-92 India emerged as one of the fastest growing economy of the world. The rules of the WTO, signed in 1994, cover trade areas such as food, environmental standards, Regulation of services such as transport, how Government can use taxes, copyright, patent law, Agricultural Policy and more. It has to review the trade Related Aspects of Intellectual Property Rights (TRIPS) and Anti-dumping Practices. Further it is concentrating on additional issues like Foreign Direct Investment, Competition Policy, Environmental Safety, Health and Labour standards.

Reflecting the regions recent economic reforms, South Asian Economies fared well since 1996, with most countries achieving healthy GDP and export growth rates, improved creditworthiness indicators and increased foreign investment. Despite these achievements, the region still contributes only one per cent of world trade and attracts less foreign investment than other regions. South Asian Countries to be a strong performer. Growth in 1998 and 1999 was 6.2 and 5.5 per cent respectively. In India, the industrial sector is showing signs of a pickup after three years of sluggish performance and GDP growth was 5.9 per cent in 1999. Pakistan's continued political instability, weak agriculture performance and macro economic imbalances constrained growth to 3.1 per cent in 1999. In Bangladesh, severe floods hampered agriculture and manufacturing sector activity, which led to a decline in GDP growth to 4.4 per cent in 1999. Declining industrial output slowed growth in Sri Lanka to 4.2 per cent in 1999 from 4.7 per cent in 1998. Pakistan's GDP growth of 4.8 per cent in 2000 was the highest since 1997, and was the result of a strong agriculture sector and an increase in exports. Bangladesh also recovered well from moderate growth in 1999, when floods devasted the country. Other countries in the sub-region showed generally strong signs of recovery during the year, attributed largely to higher agricultural growth.

Inflation was generally kept under control in the sub-region, although in India the wholesale price index rose to 7 per cent in 2000 from 3.3 per cent in 1999. Higher world oil prices were the primary cause of this spike. The export sector played a key role in the sub-regions economic recovery. Following moderate growth of about 11.6 per cent in 1999, India's export improved further by about 17 per cent in 2000, helped by faster global trade expansion and by depreciation of the rupee.

The paper is organized into four sections. The first section explains briefly the South Asia Trade in WTO, the second section discusses GATT–WTO and the Indian reform process, and section third focuses on the WTO issues for India, last section comments on the WTO and India's External Sector. The paper heavily depends upon secondary data.

South Asia in WTO

One of the key objectives of a regional grouping is, taking a collevtive position on agreeable issues at regional fora. In the WTO, we find various such regional groups such as EU, ASEAN, MERCOSUR etc. Likewise, geographically scattered nations can group together to voice their concerns, and in the WTO. we find the Cairns Group, Least Developed Countries (LDCs), Like-Minded group (LMG) of countries, and so on. Such, groupings act as strong lobbies to exert pressure on the decision making process of the WTO, which is based on consensus.

The SAARC Commerce Ministers met in Bandos Island, Maldives on 9th August 1999 and were of the firm view that there was a move to overload the WTO agenda with new issues such as social clauses, environment, governance, labour standards, etc. With regard to the TRIPS Agreement, the Ministers sought extension of the moratorium on applicability of the non-violation clause, as also a finite extension of the transition period for implementation of the provision of TRIPS for the developing countries. Similarly, they sought extension of the transition periodnfor developing countries with respect to Trade Related Investment Measures (TRIMS). Among other measures, the Commerce Ministers desired duty-free access of LDGs on an autonomous basis. On the basis of this thinking, a common statement was prepared for the third WTO Ministerial meeting that took place in Seattle U.S.A. in November/December 1999. The Commerce Ministers and Heads of Delegation of the Member Countries of SAARC met again in New Delhi in August 2001 with a view to consulting and coordinating their national positions in the context of the fourth WTO Ministerial meeting in Doha, Qatar during November 2001. In a joint Statement, they reiterated their strong plea for the resolution of the implementation concerns raised by developing countries.

However, what is clear is that the number of cross cutting issues among South Asian countries have considerably reduced after Doha. The WTO negotiations amply demonstrate that when countries forge alliances they can generate synergy and become powerful players. Today, India stands as the leading voice for the developing countries in the WTO. This was amply demonstrate in Doha where India acted very effectively, and used the collective muscle of the LMG to wrest concessions from developed countries, and in Cancun where India took a lead in forming and and maintaining strong and effective alliances with developing nations to push certain issues to the center stage.

GATT-WTO and the India Reform Process

The India economy has experienced a major transformation during the decade of the 1990s. It has undertaken various unilateral economic reforms since 1991 and apart from their impact the economy also had to reorient it to the changing multilateral trade discipline within the newly written GATT-WTO framework. The unilateral trade policy measures have encompassed exchange-rate policy, foreign in vestment , external borrowing, import licensing, custom tariffs, and export subsidies. The multilateral aspect of India's trade policy refers to India's WTO commitments regarding trade in goods and services, trade–related investment measures, and intellectual property right.

Unilateral Reforms

The Indian Government initiated a major program of economic reform and liberalization in 1991, reversing a policy direction followed for decades. Since then, successive Governments have progressively reduced tariff protection and relaxed and simplified India's restrictive import licensing regime. Internal reforms have included reduced control over location and industrial licensing controls, in addition to some loosening of controls on administered prices in some sectors. In this process, however the policy focus was principally on liberalization of capital goods and inputs for industry, to encourage domestic and export-oriented growth: by and large, imports of consumer goods remained regulated. The balance of payments situations also improved greatly. To build on this success, India has recognized the need to continue the economic reform process, with an increased emphasis now on improving infrastructure, which appears to be a major constraint on the growth of industrial activity and export; further liberalizing trade through reductions in tariffs and non-tariff measures; reforming the subsidy structure; and restructuring public sector enterprises, which continue to be a fiscal drain.

These reforms are reinforced by the Exim policy for 2002-07 which has as its main objectives: *(i)* To facilitate sustained growth in exports to attain a share of at least 1% of global merchandise trade, *(ii)* To stimulate sustained economic growth by providing access to essential raw materials, intermediates, components, consumables and capital goods required for augmenting production and providing services, *(iii)* To enhance the technological strength and efficiency of Indian agriculture, industry and services thereby improving their competitive strength, while generating new employment opportunities, and to encourage the attainment of internationally accepted standards of quality; *(iv)* To provide consumers with good quality goods and services at internationally competitive prices while at the same time creating a level playing field for the domestic producers. Moreover, the Eighth Five year plan (1992-97), called for the movement of India's trade policy regime "to wards greater openness and to reap the full benefits of international trade". This has been Sought to be achieved through *(i)* a reduction of the "negative" list of imports and exports, *(ii)* a gradual reduction in the level of tariff rates, and *(iii)* other trade policy reforms.

Multilateral Commitments

Under the General Agreement on Trade in Services (GATS), India has made commitments in 33 activities (compared with an average of 23 for developing countries) out of a total of 161. In terms of WTO tariff commitments, India has bound 67 per cent of its tariffs in manufacturing and 100 per cent in agriculture in consequence of its Uruguay Round commitments. India also took part in the Information Technology Agreement. India's anti-dumping and countervailing legislations have been amended in line with relevant WTO Agreements. With respect to Intellectual property Rights (IPR), India's Copyright Law was amended in 1994 in accordance with its obligations under the TRIPS Agreement. India plans to make use of the transition period available to developing member countries of the WTO to implement other changes to its IPR. India's WTO Commitments can be analysed under the following categories.

Merchandise Trade

Recognizing the important linkages between trade and economic growth, the government has simplified the tariff, eliminated quantitative restrictions on imports, and reduced export restrictions. It plans to further simplify and reduce the tariff. However, the level of protection through the tariff remains relatively high and the anti-export bias inherent in imports and other constraints still remain. To help counteract this anti-export bias, export promotion measures have gained in importance. The Government has recently announced a further increase in these measures and plans to continue reforms of the tariff and other taxes. Removal of quantitative restriction on imports maintained for balance-of-payment reasons has been reached by India. As a result custom tariff has become the main form of border protection. There have been significant recent efforts to rationalize the tariffs. Tariffs are relatively high, but the average MFN rate fell from 35.3% to 32.3% between 1997/98 and 2001/02 and is expected to fall further to 29% as the peak rate of tariff is reduced from 35% to 30%. The Government announced recently that it intends to simplify and lower the tariff to two tiers by 2004/05; 10% for raw materials, intermediates and components, and 20% for final products. As a result of additional bindings taken by India in the WTO, the share of tariff lines that are bound has increased from 67% to 72%. The average (Final) bound rate is 50.6%, higher then the applied MFN rate. As part of its policy to encourage export, the Government is planning to confine export restrictions to a few sensitive items, as announced by the EXIM policy 2002-2007.

Services

The services sector accounts for about 40% of India's GDP, 25% of employment and 30% of export earnings. Recognizing the importance of the services sector in achieving higher economic growth, the government is giving added emphasis to improving services. India's Commerce Ministry announced that India would open a few service sectors to WTO negotiations to increase professional development within the country. Significant headway has been made in lideralizing telecommunications. While the government controlled corporation VSNL operates as the exclusive provider of international long-distance services, private investors in joint ventures are allowed to provide intra-voice telephone services in various States. Many value added services–including voice mail, radio paging and cellular mobile telephone–are now open to 49 per cent foreign participation. In the area of financial services, the banking sector remains fairly closed to foreign participation while the insurance sector is begin privatized. Other services areas such as shipping, roads, ports and air are beginning to open up.

Agriculture

During the Uruguay Round, India bound its agricultural tariffs at ceiling rates ranging from 0 to 300 per cent. It reality, applied rates for 1997/98 are considerably lower, averaging 26 per cent for the sector, with a peak of 45 per cent. Although tariff reforms have resulted in average duties in the food sector be in halved since 1993 currently around 29 per cent for food products and 134 per cent for beverages), industrial and import licensing restrictions continue to be maintained for a number of industries. In addition, a number of products are reserved for production by the small-scale sector. Production by the food manufacturing sector has grown rapidly, especially following increased foreign investment where up to 51 and 100 per cent of participation is allowed automatically for foreigners and non-resident Indians, except for products reserved for the small scale sector.

Trade Related Investment Measures (TRIMS)

Since export growth depends on the existence of a strong

production base in thrust sectors, which could expand to meet further growth needs, the stimulus in such thrust areas has been provided by streamlining the procedures for foreign investment. The foreign investment promotion Board (FIPB) has been revamped to make the rules and regulations pertaining to foreign investment more transparent. The first-ever guidelines for approving FDI by the FIPB have been announced to expedite approval of foreign investments In areas not covered under automatic approval priority areas for allowing 100% foreign equity have been spelt out. India has already notified the trade related investment measures main tained by it in terms of Articles 2 and 5 of the TRIMs Agreement and the illustrative list annexed to the TRIMs agreement.

Infrastructure Sector

Removing Infrastructure bottlenecks has been another key component of the trade reforms package. A telecom Regulatory authority was established in March 1997, which will separate the regulatory functions from policy formulation and operational functions. New guidelines allow private participation in ports, investment begin on B.O.T. basis, and already approval for a private container terminal valued at Rs 70 billion has been awarded. Similarly, fresh guidelines for private investments in the highway sector have been announced, procedures have been simplified and environmental clearance and equity participation made easier. Approval has been given for a railbased mass rapid transit system (MRTS) in Delhi, and the cities of Bangalore, Hyderabad, Mumbai and Kolkata have proposed major improvements in their public transport system through the introduction/augmentation of rail-based transit system.

Intellectual Property Rights

India amended its Copyright law in 1994 to comply with its obligations under the Trade-Related Intellectual Property Rights (TRIPS) agreement. Under the terms of WTO, as a developing country, India has to implement the WTO standards IPR protection laws by 2005 to comply with the TRIPS agreement. In May 2002 India enacted a new patent law. The Indian bio-diversity act recognizes the need to reward and compensate traditional knowledge users of biodiversity resources. Although this is a welcome step with a view a to implementing the WTO agreement on Trade Related aspects of Intellectual Property Rights (TRIPS), the EU is concerned over provisions related to compulsory licensing (e.g. the possibility to grant a compulsory license for a product for the sole reason that it is imported into instead being manufactured in India) and unclear or ambiguous provisions, leaving scope for TRIPS inconsistent Practices over time (e.g. exclusion of certain types of product inventions from patentability).

Anti-Dumping and Safeguards

Anti dumping and countervailing duties are imposed under the Customs Tariffs Act 1975 and the Rules made there under. The Act and Rules are on the lines of the respective GATT agreement on anti-dumping and countervailing duties. The time limits and the procedures prescribed under the Indian laws/GATT Agreement are strictly followed by the designated authority. With the increasing number of cases, to Government of India proposes to set up a Directorate General of Anti-dumping and Allied Duties for expeditious disposal of anti-dumping and countervailing duty cases.

Government Procurement

India is not a member of the Plurilateral Agreement on Government Procurement. However, we are talking part in the discussions in the Working Group on transparency in Government Procurement set up as per the mandate of the Singapore Ministerial Conference of the WTO.

Environment

With the rapid increase in the international trade and consequent increase in cross-border movement of products, the linkage between trade and environment has become a relevant issue for the international community. GATT/WTO being the chief trade body addressing international trade issues has taken cognizance of it. Already certain Agreements within WTO, such as the Agreement of Technical Barriers to Trade, and the Agreement on Sanitary and Phytosanitary measures have addressed environmental is sues to some extent. India's approach on the issue of the relation ship between trade and environment has been that international rules should not create unnecessary or unjustifiable obstacles to international trade; there has to be a clear recognition that environmental standards differ from country to country and that the solution lies in mutual recognition of product-related standards rather than harmonization and; where proprietary substances or processes are mandated for use by international or national laws for environmental purposes, owners of intellectual property should be obliged to sell technologies or products at fair and most favourable terms and conditions.

Information Technology (IT)

During the Singapore Ministerial Conference a Ministerial Declaration Trade in Information Technology Products was adopted. This Declaration aims to expand world trade in Information Technology Products. India participated in the negotiations on the Agreement from the early stages and after examination of the implications of the proposed agreement and extensive discussions with trading partners joined as a participant on 1 April 1997. India is committed to phasing out the import tariffs on the products covered by the ITA as scheduled. The quantitative restrictions imposed on these products for BOP reasons have also been phased out.

WTO: Issues for India

India's share of world exports had declined from 2.53% at the time of independence (1947) to only 0.4% in 1980, but the reforms instituted led to some growth, with India's share in trade reaching 0.54% in 1995. However, the deceleration of the growth rate of exports from 20% in the initial years of the reforms to just 4.01% during 1996-97, and the slow down in the growth rate of imports, has caused concern. While the slow down is partly related to a general slow-down in the growth of world merchandise trade from an annual increase of 19% in 1994 to 4% in 1996, it is also, to a degree, due to denial of meaningful market access to Indian goods, and to nontariff barriers including anti dumping activity by developed countries.

An analysis of India's external trade reveals that the 16 countries/territories to whom four-fifths of our exports are directed, maintain eight major categories of non-tariff barriers restricting our market access. These are *(i)* restrictive import policy regimes (import charges other than customs tariff, quantitative restriction, import licensing, and customs barriers); *(ii)* standards, testing, labeling and certification *(iii)* export subsidies (including agricultural export subsidies, preferential export financing terms, etc.); *(iv)* barriers on services (visible and invisible barriers restricting movement of service providers, etc.); *(v)* lack of intellectual property protection; *(vi)* Government procurement regimes; *(vii)* barriers to investment *(viii)* other barriers (including anti-dumping and countervailing measures).

Amongst the import policy issues, quantitative restriction, especially in the textiles area, are one of the most important of the non-tariff barriers affecting India's trade. While the MFA is being phased out, there is a certain "back loading" in so far as items of interest to India are concerned. Another problem in the area of textiles arose with the introduction of new "country of origin rules" by some of our major trading partners, limiting the flexibility of Indian exporters in finishing garment/textile items from other countries for export to the trading partners, while have invoked such rules.

Numerous restriction on sanitary and phytosanitary grounds on India's agricultural products are often not support by adequate scientific justification. Even the so called environmental bans,as, for example, on Indian marine products harvested without certain environmental protection devices insisted on by certain trading partners do not appear to be substantiated by sufficient scientific evidence. The restrictive visa regime in several developed countries has proved to be a disincentive for exports in the services sector by our skilled professionals, especially in the software sector.

In the invisible trade, while the General Agreement on Trade in Services (GATS) recognizes "movement of natural persons" as one of the modes for supply of services, the commitments undertaken by the developed countries have very little to offer to the developing countries in terms of opening their markets or facilitating the administrative arrangements or providing national treatment in the area of movement of natural persons.

WTO and India's External Sector

India's share in total world exports of goods and commercial services has gone up to 0.86 per cent in 2001 from 0.61 per cent in 1995-96. In total world imports of goods and commercial services during the same period, the country's share has increased to 0.99 per cent from 0.78 per cent. By being a WTO member, India also avails of the Most Favored Nation treatment and National Treatment for its exports to other WTO members. As per the World Investment Report, 2003, foreign direct investment in India has increased over the last three years to 3.4 billion in 2002 from 2.32 billon in the year 2000. Some of the major developments in the external sector have been enlisted below.

Merchandise Trade

India's exports have nearly doubled to about US$62 billion in 2003-04 from about US$31 billion in 1995-96, in less than a decade since it become the member of the WTO 1995. In 1995-96 exports growth was nearly 21%, there was a slight slump in its growth between 1996-97 and 1997-98 due to the general slowdown in the growth of world merchandise trade following the East Asian crises. In 1999-2000 and 2000-01 exports picked up to about 10% and 20% respectively. There was a slowdown in 2001-02, but exports picked up in 2002-03 and 2003-04 with growth rates around 20% and 17% respectively. Another positive indicator is that the structure of our export is changing from being primarily agriculture based to being increasingly oriented towards manufactures. While the proportion of Agriculture and allied exports to total exports was as high as 19% in 1990-91, it has been gradually decreasing and is around 12% in 2002-03. Conversely the share of manufactured exports has increased from nearly 73% in 1995-96 to nearly touch 81% in 1999-2000 and on an average ranges between 75-80%.

The removal of restrictions has not altered the overall rate of growth of imports. The growth rate of imports was around 11% in 1990-91, increased to 28% in 1995-96, saw a decline in growth of around 6% in 1996-97 and 1997-98 and to 2% in 1998-99 following the global recession in trade, but picked to nearly 17% in 2002-03 and 25% in 2003-04. If non-oil imports, are taken into consideration the picture of imports is all the more reassuring. Such non-oil imports, have in fact, regisrered a negative growth rate of 7.5 % during 2001-2002.

At the micro-level also, the growth in imports has not been of alarming in nature. The import data for 714 items, QRs on which were removed on 31.03.2000, for the year 2000-2001, indicates a growth in import of these items by less than 3%. Similarly, the import of 300 sensitive items, which is being monitored by a Standing Group of Secretaries, indicated a decline of 13% during the first three months of this financial year (April-June,2001). Imports during 2003-04 are valued at US$ 75600 million representing an increase of 25% over the level of import valued at Us $ 60313 million in 2002-03. Oil imports during 2003-04 are valued at Us $ 17685.3 million, which is nearly 25% higher than oil imports valued at US $ 14048 million in the previous year. Non-oil imports during 2003-04 are estimated at 17% higher than the level of such imports valued at US $ 37540 million in 2002-03. The share of POL (Petrol, Oil & Lubricants) imports in total imports has increased from 20% in 1995-96 to nearly 29% in 2003-04 while that of non-POL Imports had declined from nearly 80% in 1990-91 to 71% in 2002-03. Import increases, therefore, can be mainly attributed to increases in growth of POL import bills.

The import cover of exports given by the percentage ratio of exports to imports also shows a positive trend. In 1990-91, while the import cover of exports was only 75% it has been rising since 1995-96 and averages around 85% between 1995-97. There was a decline in this indicator between 1998-2000 due to the fall in the growth of exports in 1997-98 and a negative growth in 1998-99, but it has picked up since 2000-01 and ranged around 85% on an average. Another indicator, i.e., the import cover of foreign exchange reserves in terms of time period has also gone up from a mere 2.5 months in

1990-91 to nearly 18 months in 2002-03.

Exports as a percentage of Gross Domestic product (GDP), which is an Indicator of external openness of country, show an increase from 6.1% 1990-91 to 11.2% in 2002-03. Similarly the ratio of imports to GDP also shows a rise from 8.1% in 1990-91 to 12.8% in 2002-03. Both the indicators show that the country is opening up to the world and is getting more trade oriented. The trade balance as a percentage ratio of GDP shows a decline from – 2.0% in 1990-91 to – 1.6% in 2002-03. (The increase of this indicator in 1998-99 and 1999-2000 was again due to the slowdown in exports.) The invisible balance as a percentage ratio of GDP which was a negative 0.1% in 1990-91 turned to a positive 1.6% in 1995-96 and further to nearly of 3% in post–1999 period. This not only shows that India has now become a net exporter of services but also that the invisible exports are steadily increasing. Because of this massive increase in exports of services the invisible balance has become large enough to offset the negative trade balance thereby resulting in the positive current balance. The current account balance as a ratio of GDP which was –3.1% in 1990-91 has become a positive of 0.8% in 2002-03.

Investment Flows

Prior to 1991, India was the least attractive site for foreign investment. With the liberalization and privatization of the economy and with the growth rates picking up, the foreign capital inflows have more than doubled from US$ 24176 million in 1995-96 to nearly US$ 50000 million in 2002-03. The net foreign capital inflows have increased six times from US$ 2374 in 1995-96 to US$ 12638 in 2002-03. Foreign direct investment (FDI) in flow has also increased between 1990-91 and 2002-03. While FDI was only US$ 74 million in 1990-91 it has it has increased eighty times in the decade to US$ 6131 million in 2001-2002 with a slight decline to US$ 4660million in 2002-03. There has been a 31% in FDI between 1995-96 and 2001-02. Although the FDI flows have not borned as much as in China yet there has definitely been a considerable increase. The share of FDI in total capital flows has gone up from just 0.3% in 1990-91 to 13% in 2001-02 with a slight decline to 9.3% in 2002-03.

External Assistance and Borrowings

External Assistance on the other hand has come down. While External Assistance as a share of net Total Capital Flows was a high as nearly 30% in 1995-96, it has declined to about 10% in 2001-02 and has become a negative 20% in 2002-03. This implies that there has been a net outflow in Foreign Aid.

External Commercial borrowings (ECB) have drastically declined in the post-WTO period and net ECB as a share of Total Capital Flows has decreased from nearly 43% in 1995-96 to a 19.3% in 2002-03. This again implies that the country is commercially lending more than it is borrowing. When capital flows are incoming in various forms like Port-folio, Direct and other investments, the need for borrowing has greatly declined. The share of NRI deposits in Total Capital Flows have been increased from their 1990-91 levels but have declined from the 1995-96 level. However from 2000-01 this share is again on the rise and stood at nearly 25% in 2002-03. Post liberalization and post-WTO the NRIs are also finding their home land attractive and safe enough to invest in.

External Debt

A very important indicator of the stability of the country is the ratio of its short-term debt to its total foreign exchange reserves. In fact in most of the East Asian Economies the currency crises of 1997 had aggravated simply because the ratio of their short term debt to their foreign exchange reserves was extremely high and in many countries exceeded 100%. The short-term foreign debt got easily withdrawn and left the countries devastated with speedily falling domestic currencies and hardly any foreign exchange to finance their imports. In India this ratio was extremely high at 146% in 1990-91 and has been steadily falling in the post-WTO period. In 2001-02 it had fallen to just 5%, which is a clear indication of the stability of the country against external shocks. As a result of this, the ratio of Debt Service Payments to the Current Receipts has declined from about 35% in 1990-91 to 13% in

2002-03 the overall external debt as proportion of GDP has declined from 28% in 1990-91 to 20 % in 2002-03, while the ratio of debt service payment to GDP has declined marginally from above 3% in 1995-96 to 2.4% in 2001-02.

REFERENCES

1. Kelegama, Saman and Indra Nath Mukerkerjee, "WTO and South Asia : From Doha to Cancum", *Economic and Political Weekly*, September 2003.
2. Schott, Jeffrey J. "Unlocking the benefits of World Trade", *The Economist*, 1 November, 2003.
3. Mathur, Vibha, *India – Foreign Trade Policy and WTO*, New Century Publications, 2003.
4. Ingeco, Merlinda D., " Agriculture, trade and the WTO", World Bank, Washington D.C., 2003.
5. Wadwa Charan D., "Post-Cancun WTO Perspectives : India's Negotiating Positions as a Developing Country", Centre for Policy Research, N. Delhi, 2003.
6. WTO Trade Policy Reviews-India, Secretariat, WTO, 21 June, 2002.
7. Government of India, Ministry of Commerce and Industry, Department of Commerce, Economic Division.
8. www.wto.org.
9. www.csis.org
10. www.timesofindia.indiatimes.com
11. www.observerindia.com
12. www.asiasource.org
13. www.english.peopledaily.com
14. www.worldnewsindia.com
15. www.indianembassy.org
16. www.globalengagement.org
17. www.atimes.com
18. www.south-asia.com
19. www.csh-delhi.com
20. www.southasianmonitor.com